The Only Alternative

The Only Alternative

*Christian Nonviolent Peacemakers
in America*

ALAN NELSON
AND
JOHN MALKIN

WIPF & STOCK · Eugene, Oregon

THE ONLY ALTERNATIVE
Christian Nonviolent Peacemakers in America

www.wipfandstock.com

ISBN: 978-155-635-262-1

This book is gratefully dedicated to peacemakers everywhere.

May all beings be happy, peaceful, and free.

Contents

Foreword

THE SEEDS that grew into this manuscript were planted early in my life, but I didn't become aware of them until the mid-1980s. After fifteen years of work opposing war and nuclear weapons, I realized I did not understand the processes, methods, or principles of nonviolent Christian peacemaking as much as I understood the processes of psychological growth and healing facilitated by psychotherapy. I had to admit I knew more about opposing violence than about making peace.

The Only Alternative begins with a brief description of the pervasive violence that exists in the United States and the rest of the world, and how we Christians often perpetuate, allow, or ignore such violence altogether.

The second chapter looks closely at the words of Jesus, the original peacemaker, and the many ways he used, advocated, and lived a life of nonviolence.

I do not mean to reduce Jesus of Nazareth to a one-dimensional historical savior. I mean to say, however, that Jesus was much more of a nonviolent peacemaker—and nonviolent peacemaking is much more central in Jesus' teachings—than most modern U.S. Christians believe or understand. Many centuries of history reveal that Jesus' nonviolent peacemaking has been seldom understood or seriously taught in mainstream churches.

Examples of Christian peacemakers in America are plentiful but usually ignored. They include Martin Luther King Jr. and other Protestants, Thomas Kelly and other Quakers and Roman Catholics like Dorothy Day, Thomas Merton, and James W. Douglass.

These peacemakers' work has been researched empathetically, as they presented and understood those Christian teachings themselves. I have tried to understand their teachings about Christian peacemaking in ways that help the nature of each person's insights, methods, and principles emerge from their own writing and through my summaries of their other work. This approach has the advantages of describing many ways of understanding Christian peacemaking and illustrating the differences in temperaments and personalities of these practitioners.

As part of their social context, many of the featured peacemakers died before modern feminists and many other women and men helped us see the need for gender equality as a vital aspect of human rights. I believe that if they had been allowed to live longer, at least most of them would favor, work for and articulate the gender equality so absent from nearly all earlier writing.

The Only Alternative explains the most important learnings from more than thirty years of study, teaching and work with nonviolent Christian peacemakers and peacemaking, beginning at Harvard Divinity School in 1970. These teachings about living a life of nonviolence are especially important now, because of the pervasive violence and threats in our nation and on earth, and—more positively—because of the tremendous personal and group peacemaking opportunities we face and the deep pool of potential that lives within and among us.

I hope the teachings in this book make Jesus' nonviolent peacemaking as clear and practical as possible for addressing today's greatest needs. We must show how applicable and powerful Jesus' teachings are for today's national and global epidemic of violence. It is important because it describes how we can make peace in our hearts and minds and between people, groups, nations, and religions. These principles can be taught at all levels of education and applied in all types of relationships.

There is much we can do for peace and life by learning and applying Jesus' nonviolent peacemaking—with grace and guidance; with the help of the Holy Spirit and the peacemaking disciples' heartfelt and faithful commitment, cooperation, and community. The Christian peacemaking potentials we face are at least as great and wonderful as the horrendous violent threats we now face.

Alan Nelson
Santa Cruz, CA
January 2001

Introduction

Alan Nelson worked on *The Only Alternative* for over ten years. In August 2002 he passed away before completing the manuscript. My impression is that he hoped to present the teachings of Jesus in a new light that would be understood and appreciated by everyone interested in transforming personal and interpersonal violence into understanding and peace.

In 2004 I was asked to complete the writing, research, and editing of *The Only Alternative*. The relationship between spirituality and social change has long been a focus of my own life and activism. This was an opportunity to further explore nonviolent social change and its relationship to the life and teachings of Jesus. My understanding of the history, theory, and contemporary practice of Christian nonviolence has been greatly strengthened through this process, and for that I am grateful. In my estimation, this book offers readers just the "tip of the iceberg" in terms of nonviolent writings, biographies, philosophies, and actions based on the teachings of Jesus as applied by peacemakers in the United States. So many individuals and organizations in the U.S. and elsewhere have contributed to a deeper awareness of the power of love and truth in action. I offer my sincere apologies to those who have been left unmentioned or who have received less than their due in the pages that follow.

In the original manuscript of *The Only Alternative*, only one of the Christian American peacemakers highlighted was still living. The teachings of Jesus on compassion, nonviolence, and direct action are in danger of losing their strength and urgency if we view them as relegated either to the past or to an impossible utopian future. In order to emphasize the contemporary relevance and presence of radical Christian nonviolent action in the United States, I decided to add a chapter on another living Christian peacemaker in America: Kathy Kelly. I chose to highlight Kelly because her nonviolent efforts for social change confront one of the most challenging realms of violence of our time—the U.S. economic and military war on Iraq. I had the great opportunity to interview Kathy twice before being invited to complete *The Only Alternative*, and interviewed her again during the completion of this book.

Likewise, I also interviewed the other living peacemaker featured in this book, Jim Douglass. Excerpts from our discussion have been included, with the intention of personalizing and illuminating his writings and actions. Indeed, if Martin Luther King Jr., Thomas Merton, Dorothy Day, Rufus Jones and Thomas Kelly were alive today I would have sought personal interviews with them as well.

The Only Alternative calls to Christians and non-Christians in the United States to keep alive, despite all obstacles, the energy and dreams of all of the peacemakers highlighted here. It is through love, compassion, forgiveness, direct understanding of the interconnection of all life, and engaged social action that peace will prevail. The Kingdom of God is now or never.

John Malkin
Santa Cruz, California
January 2007

I

Contemporary Violence Necessitates Christian Nonviolent Peacemaking

Hate begets hate; violence begets violence;
toughness begets a greater toughness.
We must meet the force of hate with the power of love.[1]

THROUGHOUT HUMAN history, violence has failed to create peaceful communities in which the world's people can live, thrive, and interact. Though some interpersonal (behavioral) or international (systemic) acts of violence and war may temporarily interrupt violence in the short term, violence always perpetuates violence. There is no way to create peace and safety with strategies based in violence. Only through means that are themselves peaceful and nonviolent can anger and fear be relaxed, compassion cultivated, and peace realized.

We have been taught to believe that a beneficial way to influence the behavior of people whose actions disturb us is to judge them and threaten them with various degrees of violence, or by actually inflicting violence upon them. This tendency to meet disturbing action with violence can be seen in the "spanking" of children, in the punishment of prisons, and in the retribution of wars.[2] Though

1. King, "Experiment in Love," 17.
2. Straus, *Beating the Devil Out of Them*, p.101–102: "In short, children learn from corporal punishment the script to follow for almost all violence. The basic principle of that script is what underlies most instances of parents hitting children—that when someone does something outrageous and won't listen to reason, it is morally correct to physically attack the offender. That principal, which is taught by corporal punishment, explains most instances of violence, ranging from a parent hitting a child, to a child hitting a sibling, to a husband or wife slapping his or her partner, to a man stabbing someone who makes a pass at

these actions may stem from a compassionate desire to contribute to the well-being of another person, all of these use punitive strategies based on the idea that the best way to influence the behavior of another person is by inflicting physical or psychological suffering upon them, rather then by discovering a strategy that would compassionately meet the needs of all involved.[3] This education that emphasizes moralistic judgment of others as right or wrong and good or bad is based in a system of reward and punishment that is applied to self and others. Jesus challenged this method when he urged people to give up revenge and war and to utilize the power of revolutionary love. He urged his followers to turn from retribution and the notion of "an eye for an eye" to a compassionate way of "turning the other cheek" and "loving your enemies" (Matt 5:39, 44).

The main strategies available for dealing with violence are to ignore it, to use violence, or to call on the soul force of nonviolence. Jesus and the peacemakers featured in this book are aware that ignoring violence does not facilitate peace. In fact, the more that people ignore the violence within and among us, the more that violence is free to grow. Virtually every spiritual tradition has offered the view that violence creates more violence, and that rather than trying to find a way to peace, peace itself is the way.

This call to peace and compassion is challenged by conditions that can make it difficult for us to be aware of the possibilities of Christian nonviolence: the quickened pace of modern life; economic, gender, and racial disparity; despair due to the perception that we are unable to effect political and social change; and a continual focus on the consumption of material goods and on aversion towards discom-

---

his girlfriend or wife, to capital punishment and war. Lost along the way is the principle that all differences must be dealt with without violence (except where physical self-defense is involved.)

3. Rosenberg, *Nonviolent Communication*, 161: "The intention behind the protective use of force is to prevent injury or injustice. The intention behind the punitive use of force is to cause individuals to suffer for their perceived misdeeds. When we grab a child who is running into the street to prevent the child from being injured, we are applying protective force. The punitive use of force, on the other hand, might involve physical or psychological attack, such as spanking the child or reproofs like, 'How could you be so stupid! You should be ashamed of yourself!'"

fort in the pursuit of satisfying our own personal desires, a view that is strongly perpetuated by external and internalized education.

All violence—personal, interpersonal, military, and institutional—is the result of an alienation from self, others, and God. It is a manifestation of the anxiety and anger that is alive when we think that we are separate beings, and that our thoughts and actions do not affect others. We have been taught to think that peace and love are things to be found outside of ourselves, in the future.

In many cases, religion and politics have cultivated the idea that peace or the "kingdom of God" are available only in the next life, a strategy that allows for those institutions—military, corporate or civil—to grow and to continue to enjoy support from those who are directly suffering due to the economic, environmental, and spiritual degradation that result from the actions of those very institutions that they are keeping alive. Jesus challenged the institutions of violence of his day with love and compassion. The Christian peacemakers highlighted in the chapters that follow have challenged contemporary Christians, and the churches that they belong to, to withdraw support from modern institutions that are based in violence. Simultaneously, they have participated in the cultivation of personal and international relations based in trust, forgiveness, and understanding.

Ultimately, whenever we participate in or enable violence against other people, we also hurt ourselves because we are all children of God, interconnected in one life. Like Cain, we are perpetuating violence against our own siblings. We are "one body in Christ," inextricably linked, even with those who may want to harm or kill us.

The self-destructive dimensions of violence are especially apparent when we remember that all human beings have God-given potentials for spiritual growth and happiness, and that acts of violence done in revenge and hatred hinder any spiritual and emotional growth. Violence prevents our realizing who we are and who we might become on Jesus' way to peace. Any violence against God's creatures is violence against life itself that exacerbates the alienation that so many feel from themselves, from others, and from the love of God.

Interpersonal (Behavioral) Violence

Interpersonal violence is the kind of violence many people in the United States fear most. Examples include shootings, stabbings, kidnappings, rapes, beatings, and physical and sexual violence towards children. According to the FBI, about 1,381,259 violent crimes were committed in the United States in 2003, including 93,433 rapes and 16,500 murders.[4] About 70 percent of the murders were committed by people with guns.[5] On average, this is more than forty-five people killed intentionally every day. More citizens are murdered each year in the United States than the number of United States soldiers killed in the worst year of the war in Vietnam.[6]

Another common form of interpersonal violence, domestic violence, occurs in families and in other close relationships. The large majority of domestic violence is committed by men against their children, spouses, or girlfriends, though some women also perpetrate physical and psychological violence against children and spouses. The psychological damage from such violence can last a person's entire lifetime. During such a lifetime, the person as well as his or her loved ones often suffer from the ongoing side affects (the "collateral damage") from the original family violence.

Many educators, scientists, and parents acknowledge that the violent images that dominate television, film, video games, and other media directly affect the ideas and behavior of children, as does violent behavior exhibited by adults.[7] American children are witnesses, victims, and perpetrators of more and more violence, with younger and younger children involved in violence with guns. [8]

---

4. CIUS Violent Crime Report, 3 (crime statistics), 7 (homicide statistics), 13 (rape statistics).

5. Ibid., 18.

6. http://www.archives.gov/research/vietnam-war/casualty-statistics.html ("Statistical Information about casualties of the Vietnam Conflict" - 16,592 U.S. soldiers killed in 1968).

7. Kirsch, Children, 210.

8. The Children's Defense Fund and the National Center for Health Statistics report: "In a single year, 3,012 children and teens were killed by gunfire in the United States, according to the latest national data released in 2002. That is one child every three hours; eight children every day; and more than 50 children every week. And every year, at least 4 to 5 times as many kids and teens suffer

The national justice system of police, courts, and prisons continues to be based in the notion of reward and punishment: the idea that if people are forced to suffer, then they will repent and change their behavior. The message from Jesus and the nonviolent Christian peacemakers is to oppose retribution and to cultivate compassion and forgiveness. In reality, our system of punitive justice, including capital punishment, has failed to reduce violence and increase peace domestically or internationally. Although over half of all countries have abolished the death penalty in law or practice, the United States continues to allow the taking of life as punishment. According to a 2006 report by Amnesty International, the countries that killed most prisoners in 2006 were China (1010), Iran (177), Pakistan (82), Iraq (65), Sudan (65), and the United States (53).[9]

---

from non-fatal firearm injuries" (Children's Defense Fund, "Protect Children"). "American children are more at risk from firearms than the children of any other industrialized nation," according to the National Center for Disease Control. "In one year, firearms killed no children in Japan, 19 in Great Britain, 57 in Germany, 109 in France, 153 in Canada, and 5,285 in the United States" (National Education Association Health Information Network, "Statistics: Gun Violence"). On November 21, 2007, CNN reported: "Three boys, ages 8 and 9, were charged Monday with raping an 11-year-old girl last week, court officials and police said. 'Never in my 20-plus years of law enforcement have I conceived of something like this,' Police Chief Michael Wilkie of Acworth, Georgia, told CNN" ("3 9-year-old boys." Accessed January 4, 2008. Online: http://orangekite .com/daily_news_9year_old_rapes_11year_old.htm).

9. "During 2006, at least 1,591 people were executed in 25 countries. At least 3,861 people were sentenced to death in 55 countries. These were only minimum figures; the true figures were certainly higher . . . As in previous years, the vast majority of executions worldwide were carried out in a small handful of countries. In 2006, 91 per cent of all known executions took place in six countries: China, Iran, Pakistan, Iraq, Sudan and the USA . . . Based on public reports available, Amnesty International estimated that at least 1,010 people were executed in China during the year, although these figures are only the tip of the iceberg. Credible sources suggest that between 7,500 to 8,000 people were executed in 2006. The official statistics remain a state secret, making monitoring and analysis problematic. . . . Iran executed 177 people, Pakistan 82 and Iraq and Sudan each at least 65. There were 53 executions in 12 states in the USA . . . The worldwide figure for those currently condemned to death and awaiting execution is difficult to assess. The estimated number at the end of 2006 was between 19,185 and 24,646 based on information from human rights groups, media reports and the limited official figures available (Amnesty International, "Death Penalty").

The thoughts and actions of the people who live within the United States are influenced by the actions of those in power; when we see our government committing murder to resolve international conflicts, we are more likely to believe that interpersonal conflicts can *also* be resolved with violence.[10] On April 20, 1999, twelve students and one teacher were killed at Columbine High School in Colorado, by two armed students. That day President Clinton issued a statement: "We must do more to reach out to our children and teach them to express their anger and resolve their conflicts with words, not weapons."[11] At the very moment he spoke these words, United States combat jets were dropping bombs on Serbia.

In 1966 when Charles Whitman, an ex-United States marine, shot people at random from a tower at the University of Texas at Austin, killing eighteen, the nation was shocked. Today such events seem to happen on a more regular basis, from the 1986 shooting spree by a postal worker that left fourteen dead to the 2003 freeway-sniper shootings in Ohio, and the 2006 sniper shootings in Washington DC and Indiana.

Media Violence

When entertainment becomes violent, violence becomes entertainment. Modern media graphically portray all kinds of violence in movies, television programs, books, magazines, Internet, and interactive games in which "players" can "participate" in explicit forms of murder and other violence. Mainstream media consistently and repetitively present stories and images of interpersonal and international violence as news and entertainment, propagating an alienated relationship to reality and enhancing the media consumer's identification as an *observer* rather than a *participant* who might effect change. In turn, constant exposure to violence, without a cultivation of compassion and understanding, often leads to feelings of despair and fear. This sense of despair and of a lack of hope in the possibility of stemming violence creates an alienation from reality. We see the images of the

10. Archer and Gartner, *Violence and Crime*. In addition, it is not uncommon for political leaders in the United States to recommend alternatives to violence for others while they themselves participate in war and other violence.

11. *Guardian*, April 20, 1999.

dead and wounded from car bombs exploding in Iraq, or prisoners in United States military jails being tortured, and we become distant observers to atrocities as they unfold in our lifetime, without even considering how we support or contribute to such violence.

Several decades of sophisticated short-term and long-term research by the United States Surgeon General and other scientists and professionals unequivocally affirms that media violence causes 1) an *aggressor effect* of increased aggression and even violence towards others; 2) a *victim effect* of increased fearfulness, mistrust, or "mean world syndrome," and self-protective behavior (such as carrying a gun, which ironically increases one's risk of becoming a victim of violence); 3) a *bystander effect* of increased desensitization, callousness, and behavioral apathy toward other victims of violence; and 4) an *appetite effect* of increased self-initiated behavior to further expose oneself to violent material.[12]

Television programming for children is even more violent than programming produced for adults. Research shows that on average there are five or six acts of violence per hour in prime-time TV and twenty to twenty-five acts of violence per hour—four times as much—on Saturday-morning "children's TV." Average children in the United States, who watch two to four hours a day, see eight thousand murders and one hundred thousand other acts of violence by the time they leave elementary school. Research shows that the movie-rating system, which is supposed to protect young people from exposure to violent images, is more focused on limiting their encounters with sexual imagery than with violent imagery. In fact,

12. In 2002, Rea Bailey of CNN reported: "The nation's first major study on the effects of TV violence was a 1972 U.S. surgeon general's report that said, 'Televised violence, indeed, does have an adverse effect on certain members of our society.' Professional health organizations such as the American Academy of Pediatrics, American Psychological Association and American Medical Association have concluded data show at least a casual link between extensive TV viewership and aggression in children." In *Science*, Jeffrey Johnson et al., "Television Viewing," report the following: "Television viewing and aggressive behavior were assessed over a 17-year interval in a community sample of 707 individuals. There was a significant association between the amount of time spent watching television during adolescence and early adulthood and the likelihood of subsequent aggressive acts against others. This association remained significant after previous aggressive behavior, childhood neglect, family income, neighborhood violence, parental education, and psychiatric disorders were controlled statistically."

R-rated films have greater quantities and more explicit portrayals of violence than X-rated films do.[13]

One of the encouraging findings of research into violence by modern psychologists, psychiatrists, and other behavioral and social scientists is that violence is learned. By observing military training, we can see that it literally takes a great deal of "education" and "programming" to desensitize people and train them as soldiers. By weakening their capacity for compassion and teaching them to demonize others, human beings can become "natural-born killers." But a reverence and respect for life is not easily diminished.[14]

Media violence both *causes* violence and is *itself* a form of violence, in that it is a psychological and spiritual assault on human consciousness that affects the thoughts, feelings, attitudes, beliefs, behaviors, relationships, politics, and stewardship of those who consume it. The ownership of mass media has been consolidated in recent years, with five corporations—Time Warner, Disney, Rupert Murdoch's News Corporation, Bertelsmann of Germany, and Viacom (formerly CBS)—now controlling 90 percent of the newspapers, magazines, Television and radio stations, records, movies, videos, books, wire services, and photo agencies in the United States.[15] Some of the media are unlikely to present information critical of the arms industry or of weapons development because they are owned by United States defense contractors. For example, NBC, the sixth-largest media conglomerate in the United States, is owned by General Electric, a corporation among the top fifteen largest military contractors in the United States.[16] Nonviolent Christian peacemakers seek

13. Yang and Linz, "Movie Ratings," 28–42. The study found that R-rated movies are on average four times as violent as those rated X.

14. Grossman, *On Killing*, 250–251. "In World War II, 75 to 80 percent of riflemen did not fire their weapons at an exposed enemy, even to save their lives or the lives of their friends . . . In Vietnam the nonfiring rate was close to 5 percent . . . Psychological conditioning was applied en masse to a body of soldiers, who, in previous wars, were shown to be unwilling or unable to engage in killing activities . . . The triad of methods used to achieve this remarkable increase in killing are desensitization, conditioning, and denial defense mechanisms."

15. Bagdikian, *New Media Monopoly*, 3. Bagdikian comments: "In 1983 there were fifty dominant media corporations; today there are five."

16. In *Mother Jones* magazine, Geov Parrish reports the following: "As

to break through the media-induced trance of violence and awaken to the reality of their potential to transform violence in themselves and in the world into love and peace.

International (Military) Violence

War has become more prevalent and more violent during the last four centuries, judging by the numbers of people killed in wars or the percentage of populations killed in them. This is partially due to the fact that during the twentieth century, the power of military weapons made a leap of historically unprecedented and practically unimaginable proportions. That was especially true in the arms race perpetrated and led by the United States and the Soviet Union in the last half of the twentieth century.

In ancient times, most wars were fought by soldiers in hand-to-hand and face-to-face combat. The limited weaponry and direct contact limited the casualties. In modern times, research and development have created deadlier weapons that can be used from greater distances, thus creating a separation between the soldiers—who may direct a laser-guided bomb to a target—and the soldiers and civilians who experience the explosion.

At the beginning of the twentieth century, the machine gun was the cutting edge of lethal technology. Only a few years later, it was thought that using airplanes for aerial bombardment would cause such devastation as to end war for all time. But they only made war much more deadly and destructive. Today's non-nuclear weapons are about one hundred thousand times more deadly than the weapons used in wars three hundred years ago.

---

both a billion-dollar arms dealer and owner of the NBC network, America's General Electric is uniquely positioned to profit from the new arms race—and simultaneously to influence what the public knows about the weapons buildup. GE had aircraft-engine sales in excess of $2 billion during 1996. That's not an insubstantial amount—but it's only 2 percent of the corporate giant's $79.1 billion in overall sales that year." Bagdikian, *New Media Monopoly*, remarks: "It may not be coincidental that during these years of consolidation of mass media ownership the country's progressive political spectrum, as reflected in its news, shifted. As noted, what was once liberal is now depicted as radical and even unpatriotic. The shift does not reflect the political and social values of the American public as a whole."

According to the Stockholm International Peace Research Institute, about $950 billion is allocated annually on combined worldwide arms sales and military spending. Between 2001 and 2003, worldwide arms sales earned $148 billion, with $76 billion of that earned by the United States. About half of all United States weapons sales go to "developing" countries, and it is not uncommon for weapons to be sold to both "sides" of a conflict—like Iran and Iraq during the 1990s—or for alliances to shift and for United States weapons to later be pointed at United States soldiers, as is currently happening in Afghanistan and Iraq.[17] Of the twenty-five countries that were involved in armed conflict in 2003, the United States transferred weapons to eighteen of them, according to the World Policy Institute. A State Department human rights report defined thirteen of the top twenty-five recipients of United States arms as "undemocratic."[18]

Millions of people are affected by military violence, which causes pain, suffering, and sacrifices that can often last a lifetime. Those who kill and injure others in warfare also cause extreme spiritual and psychological damage to themselves. When we intentionally harm others, we also harm ourselves. An indication of this self-inflicted harm is the high incidence of post-traumatic stress disorder among veterans of the United States war in Vietnam and the twenty-two suicides and over six hundred evacuations for psychiatric reasons of United States soldiers in Iraq from 2003 to 2005.[19]

The kind of mass murder and potential "omnicide" (killing all life on earth) threatened by modern wars and weapons can be seen as suicidal. From the point of view of human psychology, the modern nuclear-weapons policy is psychologically and spiritually dysfunctional. It is a strategy for "national defense and security" that offers no security to anyone, and against which no known defenses exist except disarmament, nuclear abstinence, and nonviolent peacemaking.

Estimates of the total number of people killed in wars throughout history range from 150 million to 1 billion, with at least 108 million people killed in wars during the twentieth century. At the

17. United Nations Department of Disarmament Affairs, *Relationship between Disarmament and Development*.

18. Arms Trade Resource Center, "U.S. Weapons at War"; Aslam, "U.S. Selling More Weapons."

19. Reuters, "U.S. Soldiers' Suicide Rate in Iraq Doubles in 2005."

start of 2003 there were about thirty major wars (that is, thirty armed conflicts each with over one thousand military and civilian casualties) on earth.[20]

During World War II, about 15 million men went to war. As nonviolence scholar and practitioner Michael Nagler has said, "World War II ended Hitler but not Hitlerism."[21] Indeed, no war has brought an end to war. In reality, each war has watered the seeds for future wars. Though it is security, safety, and peace that is desired by all people, the strategies chosen by the United States and other governments have achieved a heightened state of insecurity and fear.

From 1900 to 1990, about 43 million soldiers have died in wars, along with 62 million civilians. Since 1945 and the end of World War II, there have been about 150 wars on earth among sixty of the United Nations' member nations, killing between 7,200,000 and 8,400,000 soldiers (close to the number killed during the First World War) and between 33 and 40 million civilians.[22] The total number of U.S. soldiers killed in wars is about 660,000.

It is increasingly common that not soldiers but noncombatant men, plus women and children, suffer during wars. During World War I, about ten percent of those killed were civilians. During World War II, about half of the casualties were civilians. Civilian killings escalated during World War II with the blanket bombing of sections of London and other Allied cities by the Nazi air force. The United States and other Allies retaliated with the firebombing of German cities, including Hamburg and Dresden, and of Japanese cities, including Tokyo. This policy of massive civilian extermination reached its zenith when the United States dropped atomic bombs on Hiroshima and Nagasaki, Japan, on August 6 and 9, 1945. The bombs killed two hundred thousand people—almost all civilians—immediately, and one hundred thousand died later as a result of radiation poisoning.

By the 1960s 63 percent of war casualties were civilian, a rate that grew to 74 percent in the 1980s. In the 1990s, between 75 and 90 percent of war's casualties were civilian, including about two million children. According to the United Nations, two out of three of today's war fatalities are women and children. In 2001, 40 million

20. Hedges, *What Every Person Should Know about War*, 1–2.
21. Nagler, interview.
22. Hedges, *What Every Person Should Know about War*, 7.

people were displaced from their homes because of armed conflict or human rights violations. The increase in displacement and killing of civilians in modern warfare is largely intentional and is accepted as part of the strategy of modern warfare. This was seen, for example, in what the United States called "low-intensity conflict" in Central America in the 1980s. It was also seen in the "ethnic cleansing" that has occurred in Cambodia, Yugoslavia, and Rwanda. Many civilians have been killed by *genocide*, which has been defined by the *Convention on the Prevention and Punishment of the Crime of Genocide* as "the intent to destroy, in whole or part, a national, ethnic, racial or religious group" by killing, by inflicting bodily or mental harm, by preventing births or by transferring children.[23] Genocide is also a part of U.S. history with the killing of between five million and twenty million Native Americans, much of it sanctioned and supported by Christian churches and leaders.

Dozens of genocides have happened since World War I. It is estimated that in the 1930s, forty million people were killed during Stalin's institutionalized purge of the Soviet Union; eleven million people were killed under the tyranny of Nazi Germany; thirty million people were killed in China; 1.7 million (from a total population of seven million) were killed in Cambodia under the Khmer Rouge during the 1970s; fifty thousand Iraqi Kurds were killed in 1987; Between 1992 and 1995, 310,000 Bosnian Muslims were "ethnically cleansed" by Serbs, and during Hutu and Tutsi fighting in 1994, one million people were killed in Rwanda.

The teachings of Jesus have often been used to support violence such as slavery and war; the use of Jesus' teachings to legitimate violence is a trend that continues today. However, the truth of Jesus' nonviolence and love is available to all who take his teachings seriously and experiment with them directly. Unfortunately, the development of nuclear weapons now makes armed conflict more dangerous than ever before.

---

23. See United Nations Office of the High Commissioner on Human Rights, *Convention on the Punishment and Prevention of the Crime of Genocide.*

> The splitting of the atom has changed everything except
> our mode of thinking and thus we drift towards unparal-
> leled catastrophe.[24]

Albert Einstein, Helen Caldicott, J. Robert Oppenheimer, and many committed and compassionate organizations of nuclear scientists, medical doctors, psychologists, educators, and activists have warned the United States and other governments about the dangers of nuclear-weapons testing and deployment for years, some since the first nuclear weapons were detonated.

Of all modern military weapons, nuclear weapons are of particular concern due to both their capacity to kill so many people at once and the long-term danger they pose to the environment and future generations. The first atomic bomb used during a war, nicknamed ominously "Little Boy," was dropped by the United States military on Hiroshima, Japan, on August 6, 1945. It contained a softball-sized amount of atomic weapons-grade uranium, U-235. The fireball resulting from **this** original atomic bomb was three and a half miles across, and the center of the fireball reached one million degrees. Seventy thousand people were instantly killed, many of whom were virtually vaporized. Tens of thousands more were severely injured and disabled. Thousands died from radiation sickness and other effects of atomic radiation as the days, weeks, months, and years passed.

Sixty years have passed since the United States' nuclear attacks, and Japanese survivors continue to suffer and die from cancer, birth defects, and other long-term effects of the radiation. And now thermonuclear weapons are much more powerful than in 1945. Little-Boy–sized atomic bombs are now used as triggers to ignite much larger thermonuclear weapons, in much the same way that the powder in a shell is ignited by the spark in a cap. One type of nuclear bomb in the United States' arsenal is one thousand times more powerful than the bomb dropped on Hiroshima. [25]The United States, Russia, China, France, India, and other nations presently have many such weapons in their arsenals, and it is speculated that other countries do as well, including Pakistan, Iran, North Korea, and Israel. Since the invention of nuclear weapons, the United States has built seventy

---

24. Einstein, *Einstein on Peace*, 376.
25. "1954: U.S. Tests Hydrogen Bomb in Bikini."

thousand warheads, dismantled about fifty-eight thousand of them and now has about 12,500, with 8,700 actively deployed. Overall, there are about twenty-five to thirty thousand tactical nuclear weapons worldwide: enough to create a worldwide catastrophe.

Modern nuclear weapons are much more deadly than earlier weapons for two important reasons. Much of their drastically increased power comes from their improved "yield-to-weight" ratio. One pound of the Hiroshima atomic bomb yielded the explosive power of 28,000 pounds of TNT. But modern nuclear warheads can be both much lighter (and, therefore, easier to "deliver" quickly and accurately) and much more powerful. One pound of a modern nuclear warhead on a cruise missile, for example, has the explosive yield of 1,852,000 tons of explosive potential, or sixteen billion pounds of TNT. That is about six hundred times the explosive power the first atomic bomber, the Enola Gay, carried to Hiroshima. The explosive power numbers do not even account for the effect of the radiation released by these weapons.

One single large nuclear weapon now has more explosive potential than all of the weapons detonated by all of the militaries during World War II. The total combined explosive energy yield of World War II, the Korean War, and the Vietnam War equaled nearly eleven megatons of TNT and killed forty-four million people. Some single nuclear weapons currently in the United States arsenal are twice as explosive. Internationally, the known combined nuclear arsenals have an explosive yield equal to eight thousand megatons of TNT. This means that today's nuclear-weapons arsenals have the explosive power of 34,000 pounds of TNT for every person on earth. Although this represents a decrease from the height of the Cold War, it represents the capacity to extinguish all human life on earth many times over.

The threat of destruction from these nuclear weapons—planned or accidental—has also increased in the last half of the twentieth century because of the greatly increased speed and accuracy of nuclear-weapons-delivery systems. Some modern nuclear missiles—missiles that carry nuclear warheads—have a flight range that extends anywhere on earth within half an hour, with speeds of fifteen thousand miles per hour. The most accurate "guidance systems" make it possible for missiles to travel thousands of miles and land within ten feet of their target. Nuclear weapons in the United States and other countries can be accurately fired from land, sea, and air; and current research and development is underway to put nuclear power and military weapons in space. The wide availability of nuclear-weapons components and their decrease in size has greatly increased the possibility of their use by individuals and "terrorist" organizations.

During the 1991 war in the Persian Gulf, the United States military began using bullets and other armaments containing radioactive "depleted uranium" (DU), a waste product of nuclear weapons production. The radioactive nature of this modern weaponry has caused long-term physical and mental health problems for many who were exposed to it, including U.S. soldiers who used DU weaponry or cleaned up sites where it was used. Gulf War syndrome has been acknowledged as a widespread problem for U.S. veterans, stemming from a combination of experimental vaccines and medications, and from exposure to biological, chemical, and radioactive weaponry during the 1991 Gulf War.

Many of today's modern weapons and other "high-tech" products cause pollution of the earth's soil, air, and water, and endanger the well-being of all creatures that live on, in, and above the earth, including humans. Research has shown that even if another nuclear weapon is never detonated, the ionizing radiation that is released from every stage of weapons production, storage, and waste is lethal. Much of it will remain deadly for many centuries, causing more and more cancers, genetic damage. and damage to babies in utero.

Since the early 1970s, there has been an emerging scientific opinion among physicians and scientists that *any* exposure to radiation is somewhat damaging. This is why nuclear medical procedures used for diagnosis or treatment of cancer and other diseases must always include a weighing of the benefits against the risks of exposure to radiation. Part of this scientific knowledge about the health hazards from nuclear weapons production has been gained at the cost of many suffering from cancers and other serious diseases. This cost includes those people who survived the original atomic blasts in Hiroshima and Nagasaki, and the U.S. troops who were then marched in and exposed to the lingering radiation, as well as many other atomic "tests."

The U.S.A. and Military Violence

The lives and writings of Martin Luther King Jr., Dorothy Day, Thomas Merton, and the other Christian peacemakers highlighted in this book remind us that a good place to begin transforming violence into peace is within ourselves and within our own country. The United States of America is currently one of the world's leaders in interpersonal violence and military violence. Citizens of the U.S., therefore, have a personal responsibility and opportunity to address the suffering caused by the military, media, corporations, and other institutions of this nation, just as Jesus urged the people of Rome to noncooperate with systems of violence that existed in his day.

The United States has the largest nuclear and "conventional" military on earth, with about seven hundred military bases in 130 countries.[26] Military spending by the United States government in 2004 was about $455 billion, an amount that represents 47 percent of the world total, according to the Stockholm International Peace Research Institute. Our country is also the largest producer and exporter of military and other weapons of violence on the planet. The Congressional Research Service wrote in an August 29, 2005, report that the United States remains the world's largest exporter of arms to developing nations and leads all countries in both arms transfer agreements and arms deliveries.[27] Just as children learn behaviors from their parents, it seems no coincidence that the nation with the biggest nuclear arsenal, the largest military budget, and the most weapons manufacturers and exports is also among the top ten nations worldwide in rape, robbery, and murder in its own schools, businesses, streets, and homes.[28] A 1991 U.S. congressional report

26. There are also 5,904 military bases within the United States (Department of Defense Base Structure Report, 8).

27. "Recently, from 2001 to 2004, the United States and Russia have dominated the arms market in the developing world, with the United States ranking first and Russia second each of the last four years in the value of arms transfer agreements . . . In 2004 the United States ranked first in the value of arms deliveries to developing nations at nearly $9.6 billion, or 42.6 % of all such deliveries" (Grimmett, Conventional Arms Transfers, 2).

28. These crime statistics, accessed on January 4, 2008, come from http://www.nationmaster.com/cat/cri-crime. The Web site http://www.nationmaster.com relies on the Seventh United Nations Survey of Crime Trends, a report covering the

stated that the United States is "the most violent and self-destructive nation on earth."[29] The cycle of violence includes domestic and international violence, with each affecting the other.

The United States has trained millions of people to prepare for and perpetuate megaviolence without flinching. Why are we so surprised when people in our nation, and in other nations as well, emulate the example of the United States government and other governments, and choose violence to resolve their disputes and to express their frustrations? Indeed, the U.S. military has directly and covertly supported and trained leaders of other countries, who have later used their weapons and knowledge to attack their own populations and, in some cases, to attack U.S. soldiers and civilians—leaders such as Manuel Noriega in Panama, Slobodan Milosevic in Serbia, Saddam Hussein in Iraq, and Osama bin Laden in Afghanistan.

Since World War II, the United States military has bombed Korea, Vietnam, Cambodia, Laos, Congo, Somalia, Bosnia, Indonesia, Lebanon, Grenada, Libya, Panama, Guatemala, Nicaragua, El Salvador, Cuba, Iran, Sudan, China, Serbia, Peru, Kuwait, Iraq, Haiti, Kosovo, Afghanistan, and Pakistan. Currently the United States government is engaged in two major armed conflicts, one in Afghanistan and one in Iraq, where 160,000 U.S. troops are currently stationed. [30]

Military spending and arms trade represent the largest spending done worldwide, estimated at about $950 billion annually,[31] with the

period between 1998 and 2000.

29. Werner, "Senate Unit," 3.

30. On November 14, 2007, Reuters reported: "The U.S. military said on Tuesday that 3,000 troops were being sent home from Diyala, part of Bush's plan to cut troop levels in Iraq. While the overall number of troops in Iraq would drop from its current level of about 162,000, the number in Diyala would remain the same, with the 3,000 leaving to be replaced by another brigade already in Iraq, the military said" (Tait, "Three U.S. Troops Killed").

31. The War Resisters League reports that 51 percent (1 trillion, 228 billion dollars) of the 2008 federal budget supports the military ("Where Your Income Tax Money Really Goes." This same report includes a pie chart from the Office of Management and Budget, a chart that indicates 21 percent of the federal budget goes to "national defense," The Friends Committee on National Legislation reported in October 2007 that 41 percent of 2006 federal income taxes go to war ("Issues: Military Spending") Hellman, "Americans Spending."

U.S. accounting for about half of the total.[32] Since 1975, the U.S. military budget has been between 15 to 50 percent of the annual budget, depending upon on the time period and analysis.[33] From 1940 to 1996, the United States spent about 16 trillion dollars on the military ($5.82 trillion on nuclear weapons) versus $1.70 trillion on health care and $1.24 trillion on international affairs. The U.S. military budget for 2005 was about $420 billion, and the budget requested for 2006 is about $440 billion, compared to $58.4 billion for education and $51 billion for health care.[34]

Many Christian peacemakers, like Dorothy Day, have been "war-tax resisters" and refused to help pay for past, present, or future wars. It is through noncooperation with war that we can transform our war economy to one based in peace. World War II cost about $3 trillion, or $20,300 per U.S. citizen; the U.S. war on Vietnam cost $500 billion, or $2,204 per U.S. citizen; the U.S. war on Korea cost $336 billion, or $2,266 per U.S. citizen; the 1991 Gulf War cost $76 billion, or $306 per U.S. citizen; and the current U.S. war in Iraq has already cost an estimated $500 billion, or $2000 per U.S. citizen.

There are about twenty-one million people—97 percent male—in the combined armed forces of the world: 2.4 million in China; 1.4 million in the United States; 1.3 million in India. In the

32. "Global military expenditure and arms trade form the largest spending in the world at over one trillion dollars in annual expenditure and has been rising in recent years. . . .

- World military expenditure in 2005 is estimated to have reached $1,001 billion at constant (2003) prices and exchange rates, or $1,118 billion in current dollars;
- This corresponds to 2.5 per cent of world GDP or an average spending of $173 per capita;
- World military expenditure in 2005 presents a real terms increase of 3.4 per cent since 2004, and of 34 per cent over the 10-year period 1996–2005;
- The USA, responsible for about 80 per cent of the increase in 2005, is the principal determinant of the current world trend, and its military expenditure now accounts for almost half of the world total" (Shah, "World Military Spending").

33. According to Chrisopher Hellman, the military policy fellow at the Center for Arms Control and Non-Proliferation, "All told, the United States spent nearly $1 trillion on security in fiscal year 2007, which ended on September

34. Hedges, *What Every Person Should Know about War*, 4.

United States 35 percent of the military are minorities, including 20 percent blacks, 8 percent Hispanics, 4 percent Asians and Pacific Islanders, and 1 percent Native Americans. Besides the 1.4 million soldiers in the United States, the military employs another 627,000 civilians, and the defense industry employs another three million Americans. Over all, the U.S. military and weapons manufacturers employ about 3.5 percent of the U.S. labor force.[35] With so much energy, expertise, and funding devoted to building military strength, no wonder that war is a strategy so often used in our world.

Economic and Institutional Violence

Exploitation is the essence of violence.[36]

Institutional violence can appear to be more subtle than the violence that one person commits against another, but it is just as harmful. Institutional and systemic violence cause harm by perpetuating ideas that create social, political, educational, religious, cultural, or economic structures and processes that harm the majority of classes or groups of people while benefiting the short-term material gain of a minority of more privileged people and institutions. All discrimination against people due to race, religion, gender, disability, or other characteristics is a form of violence that has been cultivated through years or decades of institutional and systemic development.

Between twenty and fifty million people were taken from Africa to be slaves in various European colonies abroad, with about twenty percent of the Africans dying during the journey. Between 500,000 and one million people—the first "African Americans"—were brought to the United States as slaves.[37]

35. Hedges, *What Every Person Should Know about War*, 1.

36. Gandhi, *Young India* (journal that Gandhi edited) November 3, 1927.

37. Frank, *Historical Atlas of the American South*, 23, notes: "The three-thousand-mile sea voyage to the Americas—the Middle Passage—extracted a cost beyond human comprehension. In sheer numbers alone, the Middle passage was the defining moment for many Africans. From 1500 to 1808, over eleven million Africans survived this upheaval. The journeys brought Africans and slavery to every region Europeans inhabited in the Americas. Only a small proportion—about 500,000—of these slaves arrived in the British North America." See also Bennett, *Before the Mayflower*, 28, 33; and Zinn, *People's History*, 29.

African Americans, Hispanic Americans, poor people, women, and others have often justly accused the United States government and its institutions of focusing on protecting wealthy, privileged, and powerful groups from violence while ignoring the suffering endured by the majority. An incident involving a poor African American man with a gun in a wealthy neighborhood may receive a lot of media attention, while news of a toxic-waste dump contaminating the water supply of hundreds of poor African American families will be less sensational. Overall, there is a tendency for the media and other institutions to be more concerned with violence against the rich and powerful than with violence against the poor. International violence, or war, is often an effort by the elite to protect wealth, resources, and privilege from the majority. Again, while the images of war may draw our attention, the images of poverty are less often acknowledged.

The deadliest form of violence is poverty.[38]

Jesus taught that a concern for the financially poor is acknowledgment of, and concern for, God within them. This sense of compassion is essential for us in following Jesus' way to peace and the kingdom of God. Jesus' concern for those the world judges to be "the least of these" is present in our own living concern for the poor. The United States is the wealthiest nation on earth, yet we allow one in four of our young school children to grow up with all the disadvantages of poverty, inhibiting physical and psychological growth and learning. According to 2003 figures, the most recent available from the U.S. Census Bureau, 12.5 percent of the population—about 36 million people—lives in poverty. Twenty-four and four-tenths percent of African Americans, 22.5 percent of Hispanic Americans, and 8.2 percent of White Americans live in poverty, although this last group makes up 44 percent of all those living in poverty in this country.[39]

According to James Gilligan, a psychiatrist who studies and writes about violence as a public health issue, "Fourteen to eighteen million deaths a year [globally] could be attributed to the structural violence of poverty."[40] He says, "structural violence [especially pov-

38. Gandhi, quoted in Gilligan, *Violence: Reflections*, xiii.

39. United States Census Bureau, *Income, Poverty, and Health Insurance*; see also United States Census Bureau, "Income Stable, Poverty Up."

40. Gilligan, *Violence: Our Deadly*, 192.

erty] now causes more deaths than behavioral violence."[41] He defines "structural violence" as "the increased rates of death and disability suffered by those who occupy the bottom rungs of society as contrasted with the relatively lower death rates for those who are above them" on society's ladder.[42]

Much of today's institutional and systemic violence, as well as environmental and technological violence, is caused or greatly exacerbated by corporations that spend millions of dollars to influence our political and legal systems in ways that individuals, by themselves, cannot. Laws that protect corporations allow them to create products or byproducts that cause harm or death to people, without accountability. U.S. corporations like Raytheon, Boeing, General Dynamics, and Halliburton are involved in profiting from all forms of military activity—from weapons production to food and laundry services for troops. Many corporations are continually designing ever-more expensive weapons systems for increasing power and profits. Corporations "enable" worldwide violence without ever being held legally accountable or financially responsible for the human suffering caused by the weapons they have researched and built. Corporations that produce technology, materials, weapons, or services used in violent conflicts guarantee themselves a profit increase by creating enemies and by cultivating the belief that institutional violence is necessary for safety.

Terrorism

For the past few decades, especially since the demise of our Cold War rival, the U.S.S.R., the primary declared enemy of the U.S. has been *terrorism*. One difficulty with fighting a war against terrorism is the lack of agreement on what terrorism is. There seem to be two basic perspectives from which terrorism is defined: national and global. From a global or universal perspective, terrorism may be understood as any covert violence by a nation's military, secret police or political group against "innocent civilians," or people who are not involved in any war or revolutionary or counterrevolutionary violence.

---

41. Gilligan, *Violence: Our Deadly*, 195.
42. Ibid., 192.

From a national or nationalistic U.S. perspective, we tend to regard as terrorism the violence of any nation or group against U.S. citizens or soldiers. The wars or covert operations of U.S. institutions that have targeted civilians are not considered terrorism by the U.S. government. When violence is enacted against the U.S.—for example the attacks of September 11, 2001—the U.S. government labels the actions as "terrorist." But when other governments and international institutions, such as the World Court, condemn the U.S. government for covert acts of violence against civilians, the charges are dismissed in the United States.[43] Indeed, when nations undertake military actions that harm, threaten, and terrify many millions of civilians, are not they themselves being terrorists?[44]

The paradox is that while the U.S. government claims to be fighting a "war on terrorism," the United States' and other allied militaries have killed many millions of civilians, beginning with American Indians and continuing in the last half of the twentieth century in places such as Vietnam, El Salvador, Iraq, and Afghanistan, not to mention leaders of such nations as Iran, Israel, and Indonesia, who have killed innocent civilians with support, training, and weapons provided by the U.S. government. Just as in conventional "war," those who fight against terrorism with the tactics of war and terror become as their enemy.

Many of the "terrorist" leaders and groups that the United States has pursued militarily were originally substantially armed, trained and funded by the U.S. government. This was true, for example, of Manuel Noriega in Panama, Slobodan Milosevic in Serbia, Saddam Hussein in Iraq, and Osama bin Laden and the Taliban in Afghanistan.[45]

43. Chomsky, *Necessary Illusions*, 83, reports: "A few days after Nicaragua's acceptance of the treaty draft blocked by the United States and its clients, the World Court condemned the United States for its 'unlawful use of force' and called for termination of U.S. aid to the contras. Congress responded by voting $100 million of military aid to implement the unlawful use of force, while government officials commented happily, 'This is for real. This is a real war.'"

44. About the April 2004 military siege on Fallujah, Iraq, Dahr Jamail, *Beyond the Green Zone*, 138, writes: "Hundreds of families were trapped in their homes, terrorized by U.S. snipers shooting from rooftops and the minarets of mosques whenever they saw someone move past a window."

45. Chomsky, *Hegemony or Survival*, 112: "The U.S. offered subsidized food supplies that Saddam's regime badly needed after its destruction of Kurdish

A trend in language used by U.S. government officials, mainstream news analysts, and popular discourse is to use "terrorism" to describe acts of violence committed by nations or groups who are too small or too poor, or too underdeveloped to engage in high-tech warfare with guided missiles, stealth bombers, and aircraft carriers. By that definition, all violence perpetuated by small or poor nations and groups against the U.S. and its closest allies is terrorism.[46]

Perhaps even more hypocritically, the U.S. has perpetuated what it calls "low intensity conflict" for at least twenty-five years. This is a method of undeclared warfare in poor nations, often denied or kept secret from U.S. citizens, that amounts to systematic terrorism. In March 2003 the president of the United States and his military advisors hoped to terrify the civilian population of Iraq with their self-named "shock-and-awe" bombing of Baghdad.

Many Christian nonviolent peacemakers have challenged this widely accepted understanding of terrorism and instead take responsibility for the military and institutional "terrorism" that are a part of the past and present of the United States. Martin Luther King Jr. and Thomas Merton were very critical of the terror that was being inflicted on the people of southeast Asia. Kathy Kelly and other Christian and secular activists have protested for the closure of the School of the

---

agricultural production, along with advanced technology and biological agents adaptable to WMD. The warmth of the relations was indicated when a delegation of senators, led by Majority Leader and future Republican presidential candidate Bob Dole, visited Saddam in April 1990. They conveyed President Bush's greetings and assured Saddam that his problems did not lie with the U.S. government but with 'the haughty and pampered press.'" Chomsky continues, "Secretary of State Shultz was so enamored of Manuel Noriega that he flew to Panama to congratulate him after he had stolen an election by fraud and violence praising the gangster for "initiating the process of democracy." Later Noriega lost his usefulness in the contra war and other enterprises, and was transferred to the category of "evil"—although, like Saddam, his worst crimes were behind him" (112). See also Kempe, "Ties That Blind"; Abel, "U.S. Arms Training Aided Milosevich"; and Scheer, "Bush's Faustian Deal with Taliban."

46. Jamail, *Beyond the Green Zone*, 116, writes: "As during my first trip [to Iraq], countless Iraqis asked me why the U.S. government continued to refer to those fighting against occupation forces as terrorists. Earlier that day a man had asked me, 'Why are we called terrorists? This is our country. These are foreign army tanks in our streets killing our people. We fight against this and we are called terrorists? They are the terrorists.'"

Americas at Fort Benning, Georgia, because of its history of training and supporting police and military from other countries in tactics of terror and torture. Many view the twelve years of U.S. economic sanctions against Iraq as a form of economic terrorism.

Furthermore, recent photographs and reports of torture of prisoners at U.S.-run Abu Ghraib prison in Iraq and Guantánamo in Cuba have led to wide public dismay about U.S. tactics being used in the so-called war on terrorism that are paradoxically, themselves, acts of "terror." Abu Ghraib, a prison outside of Baghdad, Iraq, where thousands of people were allegedly tortured and killed under orders from Saddam Hussein, was taken over by the U.S. military during the occupation of Iraq in 2003. In April 2004, international media published photos of Iraqi prisoners at Abu Ghraib being humiliated and tortured by U.S. military personnel; the prisoners were handcuffed naked in piles, attacked by dogs, and psychologically and sexually abused. To date, the Pentagon has refused to release most of the photos and videos from Abu Ghraib, though one U.S. senator who viewed them described seeing "rape and murder."[47]

The U.S. "war on terrorism" gained momentum after the September 11, 2001 attacks on the World Trade Center and the Pentagon (allegedly planned by Osama bin Laden and other Islamic militant fundamentalists) that killed about three thousand. The United States responded by attacking Afghanistan in October 2001 as part of "Operation Enduring Freedom," and in March 2003, it began a new war on Iraq.[48] In 2002, the Department of Homeland Security was created to respond to the need for safety and security in the United States. But, as we may learn from the security fence and wall now being constructed to separate Palestinians and Israelis, safety is created through connection rather than separation, through understanding and not through division.

---

47. On May 7, 2004, CBS News and the Associated Press reported: "Sen. Lindsey Graham, R-S.C., told reporters, 'The American public needs to understand we're talking about rape and murder here. We're not just talking about giving people a humiliating experience.' He did not elaborate."

48. Jamail, *Beyond the Green Zone*, 128: "While the U.S. continued to proclaim to the world and to itself that the invasion and occupation of Iraq were about freedom and democracy, Iraqis and most others in the Middle East experienced it as a devastation of Mesopotamia."

The policies and actions of the U.S. government have exacerbated the violence in the world and have created the conditions for more violence, not less, to occur against U.S. citizens and the citizens of countries allied with the United States. The U.S. government's response to the September 11, 2001 attacks was one based in revenge and punishment. Though President George W. Bush referred to his decisions to attack Afghanistan and Iraq as "compassionate" and "Christian," it is not difficult to imagine that Jesus' teachings to "love your enemy," to "love others as you love yourself," and to "turn the other cheek" could have manifested themselves in a less violent and more beneficial way. Estimates of the number of civilians killed in Iraq since 2003 range from 48,000 to 654,000.[49] Over 3,870 U.S. soldiers and 250 contractors have been killed in the war.[50]

One effect of the September 11, 2001, attacks is that for some Americans, the attacks brought a new awareness of the impact that the U.S. military and U.S. foreign policies have had on millions of people all over the world. On one level, the attacks were a response to the wars, low-intensity conflicts, and control of resources that the United States has directed internationally.

The Antidote to Violence: Nonviolent Christian Peacemaking

In the last century, violence has been carried to its penultimate extreme, with the next escalation being extinction of the human being. We live in a time in between. Only those of us alive now can help stop this military march to disaster, by converting it, and ourselves, into nonviolent thought and action for peace. In the chapters that follow, we will focus on understanding and cultivating this compassion and facilitating its application to nonviolent Christian peacemaking. By

49. In September 2006 the Web site http://www.iraqbodycount.org reported a figure of 48,000 civilian casualties. In an October 2006 issue of the *Lancet*, Burnham, Lafta, et al., reported a civilian casualty estimate from 2003 through July 2006 of 654,965.

50. According to the Web site "Iraq Coalition Casualty Count" (http://icasualties.org/oif/), accessed on January 8, 2008, the Department of Defense registers 3911 U.S. deaths. This site also reports that as of June 30, 2007, government figures had reported 1001 contractor deaths since the start of the war.

exploring the courageous lives and actions of Christian nonviolent peacemakers, we can learn how to transform interpersonal and international violence into cooperation and peace.

Many people who act violently in our nation and in the world today do so in large part because they themselves have been treated violently and have been exposed to so much violence, especially when compared with how much they have experienced genuine peace and love, and when compared with how little they have been taught about nonviolent peacemaking. So many people care so little for others because they have experienced so little care extended to themselves. We have such little peace in our land because people have not had their needs fulfilled for understanding, love and connection. Strategies of violence, based in rewarding and punishing others to fulfill our needs, are not beneficial for dealing with interpersonal or international conflicts, large and small.

Everything we care about on earth depends now on nonviolent peacemaking. It is the road Jesus walked and showed us to peace, life and the kingdom of God. Following the way of Jesus, being a Christian, includes actively applying his teachings to our daily behavior and communications as well as accepting them in our faith and beliefs, in our hearts and minds. So, while our experience of the peace of Christ often begins as a deeply personal experience in our prayerful heart, it is most often expressed in our actions and work, in combination with others, to contribute to the peace and well-being of all life on this precious, God-created earth.

However the guidance towards peace and peacemaking comes, whether from studying Jesus' teachings in the Gospels or from the personal inspiration of Jesus' presence or from the peace of the Holy Spirit, it is then our Christian opportunity and responsibility to follow the way and do the work to which we are led or "called."

Jesus taught us how to make peace with our family, friends, and other close loved ones; with our colleagues and neighbors; and ultimately with all our global neighbors, even our enemies. Jesus' great teachings of nonviolent peacemaking are for all people and all times. We can all facilitate their proliferation by bearing witness to the good news and spreading it to the people of today and tomorrow.

The antidote to the violence and armed conflict in the world is nonviolence, as taught by Jesus and all spiritual traditions. Love and compassion are the tools that help us actively witness the violence of the world—to "resist not evil"—and to noncooperate with institutions of violence, while constructing social organizations that authentically promote safety, cooperation and mutual respect. Peace between people and nations is facilitated through understanding and deep listening, not through making demands. Cooperation grows through mutual aid and partnership, not by increasing power over others through domination. The force that removes obstacles to peace and reveals the kingdom of God within each of us is compassionate love. Gandhi understood the psychological processes of *noncooperating with violence* and *cooperating with nonviolence* to pervade all aspects and moments of life, just as Hindus and Buddhists see the law of *karma* pervading all our relationships.

> *Ahimsa* (nonviolence) is more than just the absence of violence; it is intense love. The Sanskrit word *ahimsa* does not contain a negative or passive connotation as does the English translation "nonviolence." The implication of ahimsa is that when all violence subsides in the human heart, the state which remains is love. It is not something we have to acquire; it is always present and needs only to be uncovered. This is our real nature, not merely to love one person here, another there, but to be love itself. *Satyagraha* (truth force, soul force) is love in action.[51]

Nonviolent peacemakers do not seek to gain victory or advantages over opponents or enemies in conflicts. They help adversaries become friends in the process of resolving mutual conflicts and establishing healthier relationships. This process of peacemaking involves religious, spiritual, psychological, social, political, economic, and ecological dynamics and dimensions. Nonviolent peacemaking engages every dimension of our lives at all levels of awareness and is both political and religious.

> I can say without hesitation and yet in all humility, that those who say that religion has nothing to do with politics do not know what religion means.[52]

---

51. Gandhi, quoted in Easwaran, Gandhi the Man, 53.
52. Ibid., 60.

For Mohandas Gandhi, Dorothy Day, Martin Luther King Jr. and others, noncooperation with violence has frequently, and most visibly, manifested itself as civil disobedience: public demonstrations of refusal to participate in specific forms of violence. Gandhi's nonviolent resistance to South Africa's race laws and to England's colonization of India are examples of the way that nonviolence, as described by Jesus and others, has been lived out.

Martin Luther King Jr.'s marches and boycotts in nonviolent resistance to segregation and racism is an American example, as are some of the large-scale international protests against the U.S. war in Iraq in 2003. Quakers nonviolently led the struggle for abolishing slavery in the United States, and Rufus Jones supported conscientious objection to military service. Thomas Merton called for an end to the U.S. war in Vietnam, and Dorothy Day linked domestic poverty with international militarism. Kathy Kelly noncooperated with the economic violence of U.S./U.N. sanctions against Iraq and James Douglass obstructed the violence of U.S. nuclear weapons production.

The seeds of violence and nonviolence are present in every person and grow in our hearts, minds, and (interpersonal and international) relationships as we nurture those seeds. We all participate in these opposing forces daily. Nobody is exempt. In each moment, we have the choice to cultivate anger and acts of retribution in ourselves and the world or to diminish fear and hatred and instead cultivate the seeds of peace and happiness, to promote the well-being of ourselves and others. The path of Christian nonviolence is a path of peace and compassion.

2

Creating Peace

Jesus and Nonviolence

> Jesus was the most active resister known perhaps to history. This was nonviolence *par excellence.*[1]

JESUS' TEACHINGS and life exemplify the principles, methods, and processes for nonviolent peacemaking. He showed us that nonviolent peacemaking is essential to living in the kingdom of God. We can best understand his words and actions by looking at his life as an interrelated whole. By bringing his teachings into our own lives, we see that we cultivate personal liberation and political freedom interdependently and simultaneously by creating peace within ourselves and in the world. By seeking the truth, loving our enemies, practicing selfless service—what Quakers call "great unselfing"—and by experiencing the love of Jesus directly, we all can enter the kingdom of God. We support the nonviolence of Jesus, or *love in action*, by developing patience and gratitude for our life and the sacredness of all life, and by recalling that all are children of God, living interdependently on earth.

Jesus was born and lived among an occupied people whom the Roman Empire tyrannized politically and economically. Many who suffered in poverty expected the savior or messiah, whose coming had been prophesied for centuries, to lead them to the land of peace and plenty by overthrowing their Roman occupiers. But Jesus came to show a completely *non*violent way to live in peace and justice, a way that would free the enslaved from their oppressors and free the

---

1. Gandhi, Nonviolence in Peace and War, 17.

oppressors from their own enslavement to hatred. Many religious people of Jesus' day doubted the power of nonviolence because they had learned that peace would come only if they could vanquish their Roman oppressors through superior power. But Jesus saw that violence creates death, whereas nonviolence generates life.

> Do not be overcome by evil, but overcome evil with good. (Rom 12:21, NIV)

For two thousand years the teachings and life of Jesus have inspired nonviolent peacemakers worldwide. Mahatma Gandhi was originally drawn to nonviolent peacemaking while he was a law student in England and learned of Jesus' teachings. According to Gandhi's autobiography, *The Story of My Experiments with Truth*, the nonviolent teachings of Jesus, as revealed in the New Testament's "Sermon on the Mount," and two books by the Christian anarchist author Leo Tolstoy, *The Kingdom of God is Within You* and *Harmony of the Gospels*, greatly inspired him. Gandhi saw that the "law of love" that Jesus described contained the same message that Mohammed, Buddha, and the Hindu scriptures—the Bhagavad-Gita and Upanishads—offered. Gandhi regarded Jesus as his original teacher of nonviolent social change, and his appreciation for Jesus' teachings strengthened his own commitment to nonviolence as an Indian Hindu.

> Truth is the first thing to be sought for, and Beauty and Goodness will then be added to you. Jesus was, to my mind, a supreme artist because he saw and expressed Truth.[2]

Gandhi popularized nonviolent peacemaking early in the twentieth century, first in the South African struggle for racial equality and later in India's struggle for liberation from British colonialism. The movement also sought economic, class, and religious equality, and the development of a united India with Hindu–Muslim reconciliation. Like Jesus, Gandhi lived with the poor and downcast of society and devoted his life to exploring the truth of nonviolence or nonresistance to evil.

---

2. Gandhi in *Young India* (a journal he edited), November 20, 1924, 386.

But I tell you not to resist an evil person. But whoever
slaps you on your right cheek, turn the other to him also.
Matt 5:38–42 (NKJV)

Gandhi, again mirroring the life of Jesus, was assassinated because
of his nonviolent peace work. On January 30, 1948, a Hindu extrem-
ist, dismayed by Gandhi's efforts towards reconciliation with Muslims,
killed his fellow Hindu, Gandhi. A few years later, in the 1950s, Rev.
Martin Luther King Jr. became a great practitioner and teacher of
nonviolent peacemaking in the United States. King's work for racial
equality, economic justice, and an end to the war in Vietnam blos-
somed by applying Jesus' teachings on nonviolence to contemporary
struggles for social change. King was also influenced by Gandhi, whose
nonviolent methods were transmitted to him by Howard Thurman
and Rev. James Lawson, colleagues who had studied with Gandhi and
his disciples in India, and then had brought nonviolent peacemaking
to the United States. King himself traveled to India in 1959 to visit
Gandhi's ashrams and meet with nonviolent practitioners there.

Like Jesus and Gandhi before him, Martin Luther King Jr. was
assassinated because of his revolutionary message of love and truth.
The basic principles for nonviolent peacemaking are derived from
the work and lives of nonviolent peacemakers such as Jesus, Thomas
Merton, Martin Luther King Jr., James Douglass, and Dorothy Day;
from the teachings of religious and spiritual traditions from different
times and cultures; and from the understanding and knowledge provided by existential, humanistic, transpersonal, and other modern
psychotherapies and psychologies.

Everyone can cultivate peace within themselves and the world
by experimenting with the principles and processes of nonviolent
peacemaking as exemplified in the lives of great teachers like Jesus.
As more of us build personal and international relationships based
on love and nonviolence, the number of people worldwide educated,
trained, and employed by military organizations and the corporations who profit from war and other violence will diminish. We can
become conscious of our own violence, meet it with compassion,
and awaken to the truth and joy of being in harmony with life.

Truth is Essential to Peace

The truth will make you free. (John 8:32, NASB)

Truth and peace cannot be separated. Gandhi considered truth so fundamental to making peace that he called his movement *Satyagraha*, a Hindi word for "holding on to truth," "the force of truth," or simply "truth force." Truth is the primary principle and means for making peace. It is the awareness of our reality; the "outer" situation in the world as well as our "inner" potentials for peace and holiness. Like Jesus, Gandhi also saw that truth is God.

Truth . . . is but another name for God.[3]

Not just an absence of lies, truth points to a way of seeing the causes of violence and the thoughts and actions that create peace. Truth that helps make peace is based in the understanding that we can know truth from many different vantage points and that we each hold a different piece of the truth. Understanding and accepting others creates love.

The beginning of love is truth.[4]

Conscience is the vehicle or process by which the human heart perceives truth. It is the primary means for knowing the infinite depths of love and compassion. Conscience is the voice of truth we find in our own hearts. Deeper than laws and commandments or Freud's notion of the superego—the internalized *dos* and *don'ts* of a person's family, religion, or culture—conscience also transcends the conditioned responses commonly regarded as "morality." The cultivation of peace in self and society requires an exploration of truth.

The greatest of man's spiritual needs is the need to be delivered from the evil and falsity that are in himself and in his society.[5]

More an ongoing process than something static or accumulated, conscience enlightens us to realize the interdependence of spiritual, psychological, ethical, and political development. The conscience,

---

3. Gandhi, *Gandhi on Non-Violence*, 27.

4. Merton, *Seven Storey Mountain*, 372.

5. Merton, *Faith and Violence*, 11.

or heart, is like a muscle; the more we exercise and nourish it, the stronger and more defined it becomes. Likewise, the less we perceive and respond to the voice of truth in the heart, the more atrophied our awareness of it becomes.

> Conscience is what Gandhi referred to as "Friend" when he said, "Don't listen to friends when the Friend inside says 'Do This.'"[6]

The ongoing processes of spiritual growth and Western psychotherapy require the cultivation of personal awareness of truth, and living in harmony and cooperation with that truth. This is exemplified in what humanistic psychologist Carl Rogers has identified as the "Necessary and Sufficient Conditions of Therapeutic Personal Change" (1957). Indeed, the primary handbook for eighteenth- and nineteenth-century Russian contemplatives, *Philokalia* (Palmer, Sherrard and Ware, 1984) means "For Love of Beauty and Truth."

> I was born for this, I came into the world for this: to bear witness to the truth; and all who are on the side of truth listen to my voice. (John 18:37)

Truth is the first casualty of war. Nuclear-weapons production, covert operations, low intensity conflict, and all violence and oppression require a foundation of manipulation of truth through propaganda and misinformation. The obscured view of truth both causes and *is* violence. The politics of deceit and untruth perpetuates fear and hatred, built on a foundation of the illusion that we are separate from one another.

> So from now on, there must be no more lies: you must speak the truth to one another, since we are all parts of one another. (Eph 4:25)

Jesus teaches that a process that is itself peaceful achieves peace. This consistency of means and ends, or of processes and goals, is an important characteristic of making peace and is central to all truly nonviolent peacemaking. Gandhi and King both compared the means to a seed and the ends to a tree, saying the end is contained within the means. Jesus spoke similarly about the kingdom of God.

6. Merton, *Gandhi on Nonviolence*, 53.

We will never have peace in the world until people everywhere recognize that ends are not cut off from means, because the means represent the ideal in the making and the end in process and ultimately you can't reach good ends through evil means, because the means represent the seed and the end represents the tree. It's one of the strangest things that all the great military geniuses of the world have talked about peace. The conquerors of old who came killing in pursuit of peace, Alexander, Julius Caesar, Charlemagne and Napoleon, were akin in seeking a peaceful world order. If you will read *Mein Kampf* closely enough, you will discover that Hitler contended that everything he did in Germany was for peace. And the leaders of the world today talk eloquently about peace. What is the problem? They are talking about peace as a distant goal, as an end we seek, but one day we must come to see that peace is not merely a distant goal we seek, but that it is a means by which we arrive at that goal. We must pursue peaceful ends through peaceful means. All of this is saying that, in the final analysis, means and ends must cohere because the end is preexistent in the means and ultimately destructive means cannot bring constructive ends. [7]

Gandhi and King had both marveled—and sometimes despaired—at how few Christians actually applied Jesus' peacemaking teachings in their own lives. "Christian war making" and "crusades" have occurred in so many nations, churches, and centuries that Christian violence seems almost paternal and unquestionable. Early on, Jesus' teachings on love and compassion were quickly obscured. Beginning in about 312, when Constantine ruled the Roman Empire, the teachings of Jesus and the will of God began to be associated with the state and the will of the ruling elite, a transformation that historians commonly refer to as the *Constantinian shift* or *Constantinian heresy*. Constantine's legalization and legitimization of Christianity shifted the teachings of Jesus to serve the nationalism and militarism of the Roman Empire by merging church and state.

Jesus had warned that destruction would follow if people did not change their ways from "eye for an eye" to "love your enemies,"

7. King, "Christmas Sermon on Peace," 255.

a prophecy that has been interpreted by various governments and churches to mean: "take no action to change your life and society; you will find the kingdom of God later." Alternatively, we can understand Jesus' prophecy of destruction as the necessary dissolution of a way of life that denies love, compassion, and nonviolence as integral to life. Jesus' warning that the world might be destroyed if people did not shift to nonviolent means for making peace has often been understood as a prophecy of the inevitable annihilation of the world. In fact, as James Douglass points out, Jesus prophesied that either we would destroy ourselves or we would create peace through the nonviolent principles of love and forgiveness that lead to transformation and action.

> I have come not to condemn the world but to save the world. (John 12:47)

According to Jesus and those who emulate him (Gandhi, the Buddha, Martin Luther King Jr., Dorothy Day, Thich Nhat Hanh, His Holiness the Dalai Lama, and many others), every person contains the seeds of truth, peace, and holiness. Each seed rests in the human heart and the more that people follow the seed of truth, the more they realize their human potential.

Peace is Within (Direct Experience)

> The Kingdom of God is within your midst. (Luke 17:21)

Talking or writing about the peace of Christ is one thing. A direct personal experience of peace is altogether something else. Peace with Christ occurs at varying levels, degrees and frequencies for different people. It is essential, undeniable, motivating and transforming. A sense of peace, love and compassion for all people and gratitude for life can even be overwhelming. When we cultivate this deep and eternal peace, a greater love and compassion for other beings becomes our natural way of living. It is not possible to hurt another being intentionally while we experience this great and holy peace of Christ in our hearts.

> For the mind set on the flesh is death, but the mind set
> on the Spirit is life and peace. (Rom 8:6, NASB)

The mystic traditions of all religions are based in the potential for direct experience with God and life. For centuries it has been through prayer, contemplation, music, meditation, and selfless action that human beings have developed the awareness and compassion that enable them to experience and create peace without an intermediary.

Developing self-awareness can awaken us to the harm that we cause through our own violence and carelessness. Awareness illuminates and, therefore, overcomes violence and carelessness—behaviors that depend on ignorance, unconsciousness, and untruth. Nonviolence involves re-educating ourselves by cultivating awareness of our thoughts, feelings, speech, and behavior. Jesus often addressed the importance of changing our own attitudes, priorities, behaviors, and policies rather than focusing on how to change others.

> Do not judge and you will not be judged; because the judgments you give are the judgments you will get and the amount you measure out is the amount you will be given. Why do you observe the splinter in your brother's eye and never notice the plank in your own? How dare you say to your brother, "Let me take the splinter out of your eye," when all the time there is a plank in your own? Hypocrite! Take the plank out of your eye first and then you will see clearly enough to take the splinter out of your brother's eye. (Matt 7:1–5)

It is impossible to end destructive behaviors that one does not yet see and acknowledge. To turn from violence to nonviolence, we must first acknowledge the effects of the violence we have supported. *Teshuvah*, the Hebrew word for this process of (re)turning, means "to return from exile or separation."

> Seeing the means of our annihilation has compelled us to seek transformation.[8]

The Gospels can be understood on four levels: literal, allegorical, moral, and spiritual. Christians who focus solely on a literal interpretation miss much of their meaning. In *The Kingdom of God Is Within*, Tolstoy cautioned against being more interested in the story

8. Douglass, *Nonviolent Coming*, 60.

of Jesus than in living his teachings. Jesus lives in us, and we live in the kingdom of God, when we are integrating moral, spiritual, and allegorical understandings of Jesus into our thoughts and actions.

Like a raft used for crossing a river, words and symbols help us on our way to peace but are not themselves the way. Experiencing the peace of Christ directly requires us to experience our interconnections with other people and with life itself and to accept the truth that we all are brothers and sisters of Jesus. Such an experience of interconnection can transform and guide our life's work and relationships.

> Peace I bequeath to you,
> My own peace I give you,
> A peace which the world cannot give,
> this is my gift to you. (John 14:27)

Thomas Merton understood that each person's spiritual life connects directly to the source of life and, therefore, to the entire human race. Such a view resembles Teilhard de Chardin's idea of the "noosphere" and Carl Jung's concept of the "collective unconsciousness." The seeds of peace within each of us are part of our mysterious and encouraging interrelatedness and unity. Unfolding personal spiritual liberation is part of a larger collective liberation.

> The spiritual life of one person is simply the life of all manifested in him.[9]

Cultivating truth and peace develops integration among politics, spirituality, psychology, and lifestyle. The dynamics of spiritual, psychological, political, and ecological peacemaking within individuals mirror those among groups, organizations, races, and nations. Martin Luther King Jr., Dorothy Day, and many others have explored the ways in which spiritual liberation and social change affect interpersonal and international relations.

> The Kingdom of God means righteousness and peace and joy brought by the Holy Spirit. . . . So let us adopt any custom that leads to peace and our mutual improvement. (Rom 14: 17, 19)

---

9. Merton, "Gandhi," 6.

All Life is Sacred and Interconnected

Nonviolent peacemaking asks that we realize the holiness of all life. The miracle and mystery of life is a sacred gift from God, the Creator. Our greatest peacemaking opportunities will grow from our waking up to life's holiness, or wholeness, and to what that sacredness and unity imply for how we are to *be* and relate with one another and for what we are to *do* for peace, for human and environmental health, and for survival on our precious planet.

> Just as a human body, though it is made up of many parts, is a single unit because all these parts, though many, make one body, so it is with Christ. In the one Spirit we were all baptized, Jews as well as Greeks, slaves as well as citizens, and one Spirit was given to us all to drink . . . Now you together are Christ's body; but each of you is a different part of it. (1 Cor 12:12–13, 27)

Chance and probability alone have neither love, nor mercy, nor creativity enough to account for the incredibly complex interrelated and beautiful web of life that exists on our planet. Gratitude for life and realization of interdependence are keys to ending hatred and violence. Martin Luther King Jr. states it clearly:

> Every man is somebody because he is a child of God. And so when we say "Thou shalt not kill," we're really saying that human life is too sacred to be taken on the battlefields of the world. Man is a child of God, made in His image and therefore must be respected as such. Until men see this everywhere, until nations see this everywhere, we will be fighting wars.[10]

The lost awareness that all of us are interconnected children of God obstructs peacemaking. The discipline, process, and way of life of nonviolent peacemaking require us to become ever more aware of and responsive to the unity and wholeness of life. War and other violence render life expendable and other people separate and less equal. Such acts alienate us from life's unity and wholeness. In his "Letter from Birmingham Jail," Martin Luther King Jr. writes:

10. King, "Christmas Sermon," 255.

> We are tied together in the single garment of destiny,
> caught in an inescapable network of mutuality. And
> whatever effects one directly affects all indirectly. . . . For
> some strange reason I can never be what I ought to be
> unless you are what you ought to be. [11]

Peacemaking as well as political democracy and psychological and spiritual development demand equality. Human equality transcends nations, races, genders, economic classes, levels of education, and all other distinctions. Human equality, whether based in sacred or secular formulations, also provides a basis for the fairness and justice necessary for achieving, building, and keeping peace. While threatening punishment and using violence can maintain some semblance of law and order, only fairness and justice can generate true peace. The Declaration of Independence reminds us that "all men are created equal, endowed by their Creator with certain inalienable rights." No person or group is more important than any other. Superiority, an illusion of the individual ego, denies the equal value and inherent sacredness of other people's lives. The illusions of pride, egocentrism and selfishness perpetuate defensiveness and violence.

Some peacemakers actually set a higher standard than equality for the development of right attitudes, behaviors, and priorities in nonviolent peacemaking. They say that we should value others' lives and well being *more* than our own. His Holiness the Dalai Lama has taught that our happiness increases by cherishing others: "A disciplined attitude of true other-concern, in which you cherish others more than yourself, is helpful both to you and to others. It does no harm to anyone, temporarily or in the long run. Compassion is a priceless jewel."[12] Experimenting with this paradox, Gandhi realized that considering ourselves less than others is a form of love. "Selflessness" diminishes the fear and suffering that selfishness causes, while it simultaneously cultivates spiritual growth: selflessness develops gratitude for life and develops the realization of interconnection with all beings.

> Gandhi used to put the matter bluntly: when another
> person's welfare means more to you than your own, when

11. King, "Remaining Awake," 269.
12. Dalai Lama XV, *How to Practice*, 93.

even his life means more to you than your own, only then
can you say you love. Anything else is just business, give
or take. To extend this love even to those who hate you
is the farthest limit of *ahimsa* (nonviolence). It pushes at
the boundaries of consciousness itself.[13]

Jesus brought his message of compassion and nonviolence for
all the children of God, not only the Jews, but for all people; even
the Samaritans and the Romans, whom the Jews at that time considered enemies. Jesus taught that *all* people are children of God; even
those who hurt, threaten, or oppose us. Jesus taught us to love our
enemies. From a Christian perspective, all war on earth is fratricide
because all are God's children and, consequently, every human being
is a sister or brother.

> Think of the love that the Father has lavished on us, by
> letting us be called God's children, because that is what
> we are. (1 John 3:1)

We find one of the most intimate and radical Christian teachings about the holiness of life and peace and our interdependent
nature in St. Paul's famous assertion that each of us is a part of the
one living body of Christ on earth. Just as a human body has many
parts yet remains a single unit, so it is with Christ. In the one Spirit
we were all baptized, Jews and Gentiles alike. One Spirit was given
to us all to drink.

> The body cannot be identified as any one of its many
> parts, but it would not be a body without them. The body
> cannot be found in any single part, but is the wholeness
> of a miraculous and sacred interconnection of parts. If
> the foot were to say, "I am not a hand and so I do not
> belong to the body," would that mean that it stopped
> being part of the body? . . . As it is, the parts are many but
> the body is one. The eye cannot say to the hand, "I do
> not need you," nor can the head say to the feet, "I do not
> need you." . . . Now you together are Christ's body; but
> each of you is a different part of it. (1 Cor 12:12–27)

13. Easwaran, *Gandhi, the Man*, 79.

All people—Americans, Russians, Palestinians, Jews, Arabs, and Muslims—form the living body of Christ. This sacred and interconnected relationship, as much as any other teaching or awareness, demands nonviolent peacemaking. We must help people in our churches and communities realize the importance and meaning of this teaching. We are called to make peace and to stop harming our Lord, to save his living body in order for other people to participate in fellowship and communion, peace and joy.

> Belief in nonviolence is based on the assumption that human nature in its essence is one and therefore unfailingly responds to the advances of love.[14]

The Power of Love

Jesus taught that love is the most powerful force in the world for generating peace, life and the kingdom of God. Jesus centered his life and teachings on love. *Agape*—genuine love—manifests and facilitates our peace and spiritual liberation. Love is our greatest opportunity, responsibility, and joy for human beings—Christian or not. The greatest gifts Jesus gave to humankind are our capacity to love and our knowledge of Jesus' own love for us. The more we love, the closer we come to Jesus, and the more we can know and facilitate Jesus' sacred love and peace among people, churches, religions, and nations.

Love is a radical acceptance of reality, an opening to truth that is not obscured by fear or hatred. It is an unconditioned state of seeing ourselves in others while considering the well-being of others before our own well-being. We experience and generate love when we realize the eternal and interconnected essence of life. The love of Jesus is the compassionate soul force that removes obstacles to peace and reveals nonviolence, the kingdom of God, within each of us.

> You must love the Lord your God with all your heart, with all your soul, with all your mind, and with all your strength. (Mark 12:30 NIV)

Jesus' second peacemaking teaching or commandment is closely interrelated to and most often expressed with the first (only peace-

14. Gandhi, *Nonviolence in Peace and War*, 175.

ful means bring peaceful ends). It says that we will have peace and eternal life to the extent that we love all other people as Jesus does. We can experience the kingdom of God when we love others as we love ourselves.

> You must love your neighbor as yourself. (Matt 22:39)

Gandhi said that love, or nonviolence, is the most basic law and sacred principle. Because all of life is linked, all beings respond to love. The love that is essential for knowing peace in our hearts, minds, and souls, and for making peace nonviolently in our personal and global relationships, is neither passive nor easy. Nor is it some dreamy idealism. The love necessary for nonviolent peacemaking requires courage and strength.

> Jesus lived and died in vain if he did not teach us to regulate the whole of our life by the eternal law of love.[15]

Agape perceives, understands, and accepts others as equally valuable children of God. Such love often sees potentials in people that they do not see in themselves. This love heals relationships, liberating people to express and realize their true nature and full potential. Such love is not an illusion, and it does not thrive on illusions. On the contrary, this unconditional love, contained in contexts of empathic understanding and compassionate acceptance of all beings, requires a struggle with oneself and others. Jesus expressed this love and understanding that we all would like to experience in one succinct teaching; the "golden rule."

> So always treat others as you would like them to treat you: that is the meaning of the law and the prophets. (Matt 7:12)

Through giving and receiving compassion and love, any of us can realize our greatest psychological and spiritual potentials. By loving others without selfishness or competition, we facilitate their personal growth just as we manifest and facilitate our own. The more we love people, the more we are able to understand and appreciate people exactly as they are *and* to support them in efforts to be who they are striving to become.

15. Gandhi, *Nonviolence in Peace and War*, 181.

Love is always patient and kind; it is never jealous; love is never boastful or conceited; it is never rude or selfish; it does not take offence, and is not resentful. Love takes no pleasure in other people's sins but delights in the truth; it is always ready to excuse, to trust, to hope, and to endure whatever comes. Love does not come to an end . . . In short, there are three things that last: faith, hope and love; and the greatest of these is love. You must want love more than anything else. (1 Cor 12:31—13:8; 13:13—14:1)

Jesus' teaching of nonretaliation, or *nonresistance*, specifically challenged the so-called law or ethic of *talio*, which called for "an eye for an eye and a tooth for a tooth." Jesus' teaching repudiates the even more violent modern doctrine and practice of responding to violence, threats, or insults with a *greater* violent retribution.

You have learnt how it was said: *You must love your neighbor* and hate your enemy. But I say this to you: love your enemies and pray for those who persecute you; in this way you will be sons of your Father in heaven, for he causes his sun to rise on bad men as well as good, and his rain to fall on honest and dishonest men alike. For if you love those who love you, what right have you to claim any credit? Even the tax collectors do as much, do they not? And if you save your greetings for your brothers, are you doing anything exceptional? Even the pagans do as much, do they not? You must therefore be perfect just as your heavenly Father is perfect. (Matt 5:43–48)

Jesus teaches us to love even our enemies. This teaching is as clear as it is difficult to apply, for most of us even have trouble feeling love for those closest to us when we think they have insulted or threatened us. This reveals our need for spiritual maturity and grace to fulfill Jesus' commandment to love those that do or say things that we do not like. With patience and compassion, loving our "enemies" will transform them into friends.

I say this to you who are listening: Love your enemies, do good to those who hate you, bless those who curse you, pray for those who treat you badly, to the man who slaps you on one cheek, present the other cheek too; to the man

who takes your cloak from you, do not refuse your tunic.
Give to everyone who asks you, and do not ask for your
property back from the man who robs you. Treat others as
you would like them to treat you. If you love those who
love you, what thanks can you expect? Even sinners love
those who love them. And if you do good to those who do
good to you, what thanks can you expect? For even sinners
do that much. And if you lend to those from whom you
hope to receive, what thanks can you expect? Even sinners
lend to sinners to get back the same amount. Instead, love
your enemies, and do good, and lend without any hope of
return. You will have a great reward, and you will be sons
of the Most High, for he himself is kind to the ungrateful
and the wicked. (Luke 6:27–35)

The spiritual growth that "loving your enemies" requires and
produces is essential to Jesus' way. We achieve no real peace without
it. Loving those who have caused us harm, as well as loving aspects
or actions of ourselves that have caused ourselves or others harm,
transforms "enemies" into "friends," and violence into peace. Love is
the only way to be peaceful and to generate peace in the world.

Never pay back one wrong with another, or an angry
word with another one; instead pay back with a blessing.
That is what you are called to do, so that you inherit a
blessing yourself. Remember: Anyone who wants to have
a happy life and to enjoy prosperity must banish malice
from his tongue, deceitful conversation from his lips; he
must never yield to evil but must practice good; he must
seek peace and pursue it. (1 Pet 3:9–12)

Some modern Christians apologize for this teaching of nonretaliation, believing that it only applies to personal relationships,
not to the "real world" of power politics within and between nations, religions, or other large groups. But Jesus applied nonviolent
peacemaking to nations and religions, as well as within families and
between people.

Jesus tried to teach his own Jewish people, as well as everybody
else, that love was the most beneficial response to the violence of
their Roman occupiers and oppressors. Nonviolent peacemakers
have cultivated the same power of love that Jesus developed, to trans-

form violence, whether interpersonal or international. For example, Martin Luther King Jr. explained: "I still believe that love is the most durable power in the world." And, "I believe that unarmed truth and unconditional love will have the final word in reality. That is why right temporarily defeated is stronger than evil triumphant.[16]

Jesus taught that we can stop the cycle of violence only by "accepting" violence without retaliating against it. Martin Luther King Jr., Dorothy Day, and other modern peacemakers all have learned that hatred cannot stop hatred; only love can. Jesus said that we should love God above all and do good even to those who harm us. We should treat others as we want to be treated, not necessarily as we have been treated.

> Love is somehow the key that unlocks the door which leads to ultimate reality. This Hindu-Muslim-Christian-Jewish-Buddhist belief about ultimate reality is beautifully summed up in the first epistle of Saint John: "Let us love one another; for love is God and everyone that loveth is born of God and knoweth God. He that loveth not knoweth not God; for God is love. If we love one another God dwelleth in us, and his love is perfected in us."[17]

Often it is by holding the ideas that we would never do what has been done to us and that our "enemy" deserves to be punished that prevents us from "loving our enemies." Peace blooms when, with compassion, we understand, accept, and forgive ourselves and others for harm done through thought or deed. This is what the writer of James meant when he said, "Mercy triumphs over judgment" (2:13). Mercy facilitates love and understanding, just as judgment fosters criticism, condemnation and self-righteousness.

Mercy triumphs over judgment. (James 2:13)

The person-centered approaches to psychotherapy depend upon empathic understanding. Nonviolent peacemaking, which can only be achieved by understanding and responding to the legitimate concerns of people and groups in conflicts, also requires empathy. In the best peacemaking, people come to understand each other's needs and feel-

16. King, "Most Durable Power," 11; King, "Nobel Prize," 226.
17. King, "Christmas Sermon," 242.

ings. Marshall Rosenberg, the founder of Nonviolent Communication, has based his work on this power of compassion. Cultivating compassion and empathy requires a persistent and patient practice of always returning to love, understanding. and forgiveness.[18]

> Then Peter went up to him and said, "Lord, how often must I forgive my brother if he wrongs me? As often as seven times?" Jesus answered, "Not seven, I tell you, but seventy-seven times." (Matt 18:21–22)

Our willingness and ability to acknowledge regret about our violence and the violence of our family, group, nation, religion, gender, or race reveal awareness, truthfulness, and growth. The "judging mind" that accuses, categorizes, and punishes is itself violent and can be transformed through love and empathy. Jesus reveals the ultimate example of transformation through empathy in his request for forgiveness of those about to kill him on the cross.

> Father, forgive them; they do not know what they are doing. (Luke 23:34)

Repentance and forgiveness help us shed the burdens of the harm we have caused, and that others have caused us. Then we can begin again, renewed, to feel, know, and generate more love and peace. Then our heart opens again to the love, presence, and peace of Christ.

> Hatred can never put an end to hatred; love alone can. This is an unalterable law. (Easwaran, *The Dhammapada* 1:5–6)

From Selfish to Selfless

> Where do these wars and battles between ourselves first start? Isn't it precisely in the desires fighting inside your own selves? You want something and you haven't got it,

---

18. Rosenberg, *Nonviolent Communication*, 92, writes: "The presence that empathy requires is not easy to maintain. 'The capacity to give one's attention to a sufferer is a very rare and difficult thing; it is a miracle,' asserts French writer Simone Weil."

so you are prepared to kill. You have an ambition that
you cannot satisfy; so you fight to get your way by force.
(James 4:1–2)

Selfish desires cause violence everywhere they arise, from the mind
to the home, from the street to the battlefield. The painful irony is
that rather than recognizing attachment to self as the cause of suffering, much of modern psychology, politics, education, economics,
culture, and religion cultivate thoughts and actions that *strengthen*
our selfishness. We are taught to believe that if our personal desires
are fulfilled, then we will be happy. However, the world's wisdom traditions see self-centered actions and thoughts as psychological delu-
sions that create obstacles on the path of peace. In *The Dhammapada*,
the Buddha reminds us:

> Those who are selfish suffer in this life and in the next.
> They suffer seeing the results of the evil they have done
> and more suffering awaits them in the next life. But
> those who are selfless rejoice in this life and in the next.
> They rejoice seeing the good that they have done and
> more joy awaits them in the next life. (Easwaran, *The
> Dhammapada* 1:17–18).

Selfishness is one of the most serious illusions because of the
subtle yet powerful ways it solidifies the false notion that we are
separate from each other and that the well being of "myself" is more
important than the well being of "others." The more absorbed we are
in ourselves, the more we tend to regard as real only that which affects our personal interests. Likewise, we may tend not to understand
the effects of our words and actions on other people because we may
not perceive those effects as real. The Christian tradition has taught
that the path of peace requires moving from selfishness to selflessness. Christianity sometimes teaches of "selfishness" as "pride." For
instance, Paul writes: "Nobody should seek his own good, but the
good of others" (1 Cor 10:24), and today we use terms like "egocentrism" or "self-centeredness."

Selfishness can even become a characteristic of entire groups
of people in the form of national selfishness. Indeed, many nations
have elevated nationalism and self-interest to the primary guiding
principles of foreign relations.

Jesus offers the solution of detachment from our personal cravings in "the world," a Christian phrase that means "attachment to our selfish desires." Love and compassion free us from suffering because of our own desires. When we consider the needs of others to be as important, or more important, than our own needs, then we do not feel the need to harm others or to condone, support, or allow such harm to occur. Then we will see, as Jesus did, that harming others always harms us too. Martin Luther King Jr. articulated the positive aspect of this principle when he said: "We are inevitably our brother's keeper because we are our brother's brother."[19]

> This has taught us love—that he gave up his life for us;
> and we, too, ought to give up our lives for our brothers
> and sisters. (1 John 3:16)

Jesus teaches that the way to peace involves trials, persecutions, hatred, and suffering *without retaliating,* in contrast to the hope some hold—that we can find peace without accepting the violence that is inflicted on us, without loving those who choose violence. Perhaps that is why Jesus warned us that it is a narrow path that leads to peace (cf. Matt 7:13–14). Compassion—the ability to bring awareness and love to the suffering of self and other—is a cornerstone of the life and teachings of Jesus.

> You will be hated by all men on account of my name;
> but the man who stands firm to the end will be saved.
> (Matt 10:22)

Many of Jesus' original hearers, perhaps like many Christians today, hoped to achieve peace through retaliation, by meeting violence with violence, to make peace without having to suffer. On a psychological level, we begin to suffer when we abandon our self-interest. The ego responds as if by habit, trying to strengthen the illusion of its own self-centered and separate existence. Jesus taught that those who are fighting to hold on to the illusion of their own self-importance and separateness may respond to the revolutionary force of love and compassion—the powers that transform selfishness into selflessness—with fear and anger.

19. King, *Where Do We Go From Here?* 626.

You will be betrayed even by parents and brothers, relations and friends; and some of you will be put to death.
You will be hated by all men on account of my name, but
not a hair of your head will be lost. Your endurance will
win you your lives. (Luke 21:16–19)

Gandhi said that nonviolent peacemaking requires the patience
of a person trying to empty the sea with a teacup.[20] He referred to
nonviolent action as a process of "purification" more often than
"conversion,"[21] and described it as a perpetual process of *cooperation* with the nonviolence and of *noncooperation* with the violence
within ourselves, our families, communities and nations—in every
moment, dimension, and situation of our lives.[22]

You will gain possession of your souls through your patient endurance.(Luke 21:19)

Do No Harm

You have learnt how it was said: Eye for eye and tooth for
tooth. But I say this to you: offer the wicked man no resistance. On the contrary, if anyone hits you on the right
cheek, offer him the other as well; if a man takes you to
law and would have your tunic, let him have your cloak
as well. And if anyone orders you to go one mile, go two
miles with him. Give to anyone who asks, and if anyone
wants to borrow, do not turn away. (Matt 5:38–42)

At the center of his nonviolent peacemaking, Jesus teaches us to
embrace and accept with compassion everyone as they are, including
those who are violent. Nonviolent Christians try to avoid causing
any harm to anyone, including to those whom they think are trying
to cause them harm. This practice inverts the conventional idea that
revenge or punishment helps to solve problems. Without the commitment and the grace to avoid harming even those who harm us,
we rely on the unrealistic hope that a time will come when everyone

20. Gandhi, qtd in Easwaran, *Gandhi the Man*, 126.
21. Rao, *Gandhi and Comparative Religion*, 130.
22. Gandhi, *Gandhi on Non-Violence*, 29.

we encounter will agree with us completely and will meet our every need. The Christian tradition warned that disagreement without reconciliation leads to separation and war.

> If you go snapping at each other and tearing each other to pieces, you had better watch out or you will destroy the whole community. (Gal 5:15)

Choosing to not harm others gives us the power to choose how to respond to violence; not with helpless passivity but with great faith and freedom. Rather than strengthening reactionary responses based in anger or fear, we transform our thoughts and actions to help make our lives and the lives of others more wonderful. Jesus demonstrates the courageous, faithful, and blessed power of this nonviolent peacemaking in his crucifixion, as have many of Jesus' apostles and other followers in their nonviolent martyrdoms from the first century until today.

> You have learnt how it was said to our ancestors: You must not kill; and if anyone does kill he must answer for it before the court. But I say this to you; anyone who is angry with his brother will answer for it before the court; if a man calls his brother "Fool" he will answer for it before the Sanhedrin; and if a man calls him "Renegade" he will answer for it in hell fire. So then, if you are bringing your offering there before the altar, go and be reconciled with your brother first, and then come back and present your offering. Come to terms with your opponent in good time while you are still on the way to the court with him, or he may hand you over to the judge and the judge to the officer, and you will be thrown into prison. I tell you solemnly, you will not get out till you have paid the last penny. (Matt 5:21–26)

Jesus taught that with spiritual growth, nonviolent peacemaking can pervade every level of our life and relationships. He invites us to realize that we can expand our nonviolent peacemaking from the level of politics to the more subtle levels of our words, thoughts, feelings, and perceptions. We can spread Jesus' peace to the extent that we cultivate awareness of—and diminish—our own anger,

greed, hatred, confusion, and fear and transform them into wisdom,
understanding, compassion, and love.

> Even if you are angry, you must not sin: never let the sun
> set on your anger or else you will give the devil a foot-
> hold . . . Never have grudges against others, or lose your
> temper, or raise your voice to anybody, or call each other
> names, or allow any sort of spitefulness. Be friends with
> one another, and kind, forgiving each other as readily as
> God forgave you in Christ.(Eph 4:26–27, 31–32)

> Jesus rebuked his disciples and the religious leaders of his
> day when they ignored his "message of peace" (cf. Luke
> 19:41–42) and took up violence. When Jesus was cap-
> tured in the Garden of Gethsemane, one of his disciples,
> said to be Peter, used his sword. Jesus, however, warned
> that violence serves only to perpetuate violence.

> Put your sword back, for all who draw the sword will die
> by the sword.(Matt 26:52)

Earlier, Jesus had rebuked the two disciples James and John for
suggesting that they destroy the Samaritan village that had refused
to receive them. Jews and Samaritans, enemies in Jesus' day, often
settled their conflicts violently. James and John had asked, "Lord, do
you want us to call down fire from heaven to burn them up?" (Luke
9:56). Jesus had seen that they were choosing violence because they
were confused by the *illusion of separation* from their "enemy." The
desire to take revenge stems from hatred and anger rooted in the
idea that one's enemy is disconnected from you, whereas happiness
comes from awareness of the interconnection among all of life. War
and violence are essentially anti-Christian. Achieving inner and interpersonal peace requires ridding the heart and mind of systems and
habits of violence that distort our perceptions and awareness.

> Happy the peacemakers: They shall be called children of
> God. (Matt 5:9)

Giving up our defenses and judgments involves opening our
hearts and minds to others in vulnerability, trust, and love. Openness
to Jesus' way reveals that our real enemy is not other people, religions, or nations, but violence itself. When we perpetuate violence,

we perpetuate the enemy of Christ. When we disarm and open our hearts to others with love, we perpetuate Jesus' way of nonviolent peacemaking. By listening to and understanding others deeply, we transform violence into peace.

> Remember this, my brothers: be *quick to listen* but *slow* to speak and slow to rouse your temper; God's righteousness is never served by man's anger. (James 1:19–20)

Those who follow Jesus' way of peacemaking today have been warning us that nuclear and military violence contradicts the teachings of Jesus, that such violence could undo God's creation. Imagine being modern stewards in Jesus' parable of the talents (Matt 25:14–30) and having to explain why we had invested much more of our God-given time, talents, and resources in violence rather than in peacemaking.

> What matters is faith that makes its power felt through love. (Gal 5:6)

Nonviolent peacemaking requires faith that truth can triumph over delusion. Repeated direct experience strengthens this faith, and it becomes wisdom. Just as religion requires understanding of the sacredness of all life, and growth psychologies depend upon acceptance of universal human potential, nonviolent peacemaking requires faith. Awareness and truth overcome violence and delusion because violence and delusion thrive only on deception, denial, and unconsciousness. Awareness of the violent threats we face and of the ones we perpetuate can transform violence into peace.

> Evil's power lies in darkness, our own darkness. Evil's power to destroy life comes from our denial of its presence and our refusal to accept responsibility for it. The essence of our life-destroying evil lies in our unseen, unacknowledged cooperation with it. Once evil is brought into the light, it can be overcome by God's love operating in our lives.[23]

We live at a pivotal moment in history. We live on the brink of extinction. We also live on the brink of peace. No nation can con-

23. Douglass, *Nonviolent Coming*, 62.

tinue to dominate its neighbors economically or politically through the intimidation of nuclear, biological, chemical, or conventional weapons. The age of the rule of violence on earth is waning.

Peace in our hearts and minds depends on our living in harmony and in cooperation with the spirit of truth and peace that speaks through our hearts and consciences. Peace of mind and heart for us requires growth and transformation. We must make friends and colleagues out of neighbors and enemies. We must learn, practice, and teach nonviolent approaches to conflict.

Three decades ago, Martin Luther King Jr. described our alternatives vividly when he said that we no longer can choose between violence and nonviolence, but between nonviolence and nonexistence.[24] Humanity will either undergo the psychological, social, and spiritual growth and transformation necessary for peace, health, and survival, or the cycle of violence will kill us all. What we do and what we are amounts to a vote for which way we turn.

We find the way to peace, health, growth, and life in the nonviolent teachings of Jesus. We can follow Jesus, as have Thomas Kelly, Rufus Jones, Dorothy Day, Martin Luther King Jr., Thomas Merton, James Douglass and Kathy Kelly, or we can hold on to the coattails of those who practice violence telling us they will protect us from the very violence they perpetuate.

> I have told you all this so that you may find peace in me.
> In the world you will have trouble, but be brave; I have
> conquered the world. (John 16:33)

24. King, "American Dream," 215.

3

Rufus Jones, Thomas Kelly,
and the Quakers

> The Quaker's supreme loyalty . . . is to that way of life,
> which has peace as its essence. It is not merely objection to
> war and refusal to take a person's life that characterize the
> "experiment," though those are both very real attitudes.
> It is a high resolve to manifest a spirit of love and to ex-
> hibit a type of life, which if they became general among
> men would make war unnecessary, and even impossible.
> The whole basis of the "experiment" is positive.[1]

THE MOVEMENT to create the Quakers—more formally known as
the Religious Society of Friends—began in England in the mid-
1600s. A leather worker and shepherd named George Fox (1624–1691)
led in developing this new Christian way of gathering, studying, praying, and taking action. The first Quakers emphasized the importance
of personal guidance and direct experience of the teachings of Jesus.
From their early days, the Quakers challenged the authority and dogma
of church and state, and they questioned the notion that a minister or
intermediary was necessary to know God. Quakers have often suffered
imprisonment, confiscation of property, and death in their struggles
for freedom and justice. Fox wrote in his Journal that he was frequently
beaten or forced out of a town after verbally challenging clergy about
matters regarding faith and politics.

Fox encouraged William Penn (1644–1718) to establish a colony in North America where a "holy experiment" could take shape. In

---

1. Fosdick, *Rufus Jones*, 267.

1681, King Charles II of England had settled a debt owed to Penn's father by granting to William Penn ownership of a vast area of land in America. Penn left for America on August 13, 1682, to set up the colony with thousands of other Quakers who shared a vision of creating a community where they could worship as they chose without persecution by the British government or the Catholic Church. The "Holy Experiment" became known as Pennsylvania. There are currently about 300,000 Quakers worldwide.[2]

Relations between Quakers and American Indians were peaceful, especially compared to the bloody history between American Indians and most other early Christian and non-Christian immigrant groups. Also, the Religious Society of Friends has always worked for equal rights for women, regarding women and men as equal children of God and equally capable of public ministry and of filling leadership roles in the Quaker community and church.

Quakers were among the first to oppose slavery in the United States and to prohibit it among their members. Quakers in Germantown, Pennsylvania, protested slavery as early as 1688. John Woolman (1720–1772), a colonial Quaker, opposed and helped to eradicate slavery among Quakers in the United States. His remarkable journal recounts his devotion to the Holy Spirit's guidance, which opened great insight to him and supported his commitment to not engage in any consumption, travel, or recreation that brought harm or exploitation to any people.[3]

Another Quaker, Levi Coffin (1789–1877), was called "the president of the Underground Railroad" because, using their home as a safe house, he and his wife and family helped about three thousand slaves escape to freedom. It was said that Levi Coffin "never lost a passenger on the Underground Railroad," although many arrived wounded, on the run, and with nothing of their own.[4] Coffin gave escaped slaves food, shelter, medical care, and safe transportation. Such revolutionary social action was not popular with landowners, slaveholders, or some Quakers, who deemed Coffin's actions "too radical." In spite of death threats and attacks on their home, Levi

2. http://www.adherents.com/adh_branches.html#Christianity, accessed February 19, 2008

3. Moulton, *Journal and Major Essays of John Woolman.*

4. Commager, *Crusaders for Freedom*, 77.

Coffin and his family continued their liberating work rooted in Christian nonviolence to help ex-slaves begin new lives, free from their former "owners."

Throughout the twentieth century, Quakers have opposed wars and other violence of the U.S. government. Many refused to serve in the military during World Wars I and II, and they have done much to establish strategies and networks to support conscientious objection to military service. After the First World War, Quakers were among the first and most committed in helping to feed, clothe, house, and assist people in the defeated countries.

During World War II, Quakers helped to lay down another "Underground Railroad," this time to help Jews and other potential Holocaust victims who faced Nazi extermination camps. The Underground Railroad for ex-slaves served as a model for helping Jews, Gypsies, socialists, and others escape the Nazi violence. The American Friends Service Committee (AFSC), cofounded by Rufus Jones in 1917, along with its British counterpart, received the Nobel Prize for Peace in 1947 for "silent help from the nameless to the nameless."[5]

Quakers were among the few U.S. citizens to oppose the internment of Japanese Americans in relocation camps during World War II. When that war ended, Quakers were again among the first to help "enemy" nations such as Japan and Germany begin to put their war-shattered lives, cities, and countries back together. During the U.S. war in Vietnam, Quakers and the AFSC led the way in educating people about the facts of that war and the dubious excuse for the United States' military engagement. Though Christian peacemaking is integral to the Quaker way of life, not all Quakers agree about opposing wars. But no other Christian denomination or organization of a comparable size has such a consistent record of faithful commitment to nonviolent peacemaking that Jesus taught and exemplified. Quakers have been committed to nonviolent peacemaking since more than a century before the American Revolution. Only a couple smaller churches—the Mennonites and the Brethren—have similar histories of committed Christian peacemaking.

In 1915, one year after British Quaker Henry Hodgekin and German chaplain Freidrich Siegmund-Schultze met in Switzerland at a conference of Christians who hoped to prevent the outbreak

5. Jahn, 1947 Nobel award speech.

of war in Europe, they founded the Fellowship of Reconciliation (FOR). Though unsuccessful in forestalling World War I, FOR has become an international and interfaith organization, with groups in forty countries involved in humanistic nonviolent action.

Rufus Jones

Rufus Jones was born in South China, Maine, on January 25, 1863, into a poor family committed to Quaker ideals. On the day of his birth, Rufus's Aunt Peace, his father's older sister, had a prophetic vision and announced, "This child will one day bear the message of the gospel to distant lands and to peoples across the sea."[6] As he grew up, Rufus viewed his aunt as a saint and listened intently to her stories of travels to Quaker meetings in Ohio and Iowa. Quaker Friends often visited the Jones family, creating an interconnected religious community and sharing travel stories that informed and entertained young Rufus. When "a concern" called them to do so, Friends traveled. From his family and from the visitors his family received, Rufus Jones experienced living examples of the intimate relationship possible with God through "immediate divine guidance." He noted in "Finding the Trail of Life":

> While I was too young to have any religion of my own,
> I had come to a home where religion kept its fires always
> burning. We had very few "things," but we were rich in
> invisible wealth.[7]

The Jones family began each day by coming together to hear their mother read a chapter from the Bible, and began each meal with a prayer of thanksgiving. Jones grew up with a sense of reverence for the internal, spiritual world, sensing that it was as real and as important to attend to as the material world. Religion in the Jones family was a verb—an action participated in personally and directly—not something that was done for one by someone else. Social, political or spiritual "concerns" were welcomed during meetings where friends gathered in silence, leaving spaciousness that allowed for a connection with the spirit to manifest itself. Through

6. Jones, Rufus. *Finding the Trail of Life*, 22.

7. Quoted in Steere, *Quaker Spirituality*, 18.

direct experience, Quakers discovered that liberation from fear and cultivation of freedom comes in an active communion with God. Rufus Jones noted:

> When I first began to think of God I did not think of him as very far off. At meeting some of the Friends who prayed shouted loud and strong when they called upon him, but at home he always heard easily and he seemed to be there with us in the living silence. My first steps in religion were thus acted. It was a religion which we did together.[8]

Early on, Jones recognized the importance of silence at meetings. Even business meetings were conducted as spiritual affairs, with voting replaced by consensus decision making that allowed every person to speak to an issue as they saw necessary. Jones experienced the silence as a condition where one could experience a deeper awareness beyond thought.

> Almost nothing was said in the way of instructing me. We all joined together to listen for God and then one of us talked to him for the others.[9]

At the age of ten, Jones almost lost his leg and came close to losing his life. Unable to walk for nine months, he came to recognize the deep love of his mother, who cared for him unconditionally. He read the Bible aloud to his mother during this period of recovery.

> But as greatly as I loved the Bible and devoutly as I believed in my first years that it was to be taken in literal fashion, I am thankful to say that I very early caught the faith and insight, which George Fox and other Quaker leaders had taught, that God is always revealing himself, and that truth is not something finished, but something unfolding as life goes forward.[10]

Jones became a respected historian of the Religious Society of Friends and wrote hundreds of articles, editorials, and pamphlets, as well as over fifty-six books including *Pathways to the Reality of God*,

8. Quoted in Steere, *Quaker Spirituality*, 19.
9. Ibid., 19.
10. Ibid., 65.

The Faith and Practice of the Quakers and *Social Law in the Spiritual World*. He edited and helped to write a six-volume history of the Religious Society of Friends. In his ministry, writing, and activities, Jones highlighted an affirmative mysticism: the potential for all people to "wake up" and experience a direct connection with the power of love. He believed this connection was available to all and, although simply unknown, in fact is already present in each of us. For Jones, the journey of Quaker mysticism meant a personal unveiling of this truth. He realized that relaxing conventions, rules, and preconceived notions would open him to the present moment and the reality of God, and would connect him directly with love and joy and life.

> I am convinced by my own life and by wide observa-
> tion of children that mystical experience is much more
> common than is usually supposed. Children are not
> so absorbed as we are with things and with problems.
> They are not so completely organized for dealing with
> the outside world as we older persons are. They do not
> live by cut and dried theories. They have more room for
> surprise and wonder. They are more sensitive to intima-
> tions, flashes and openings.[11]

In *The Luminous Trail* (1947), Jones wrote of the Spirit as an "intimate Presence in the life of the believer" and opined that the human race will not be carried to peace by a "cosmic escalator" that will save us from the suffering of war and poverty, but that trans-formation will occur through our own mindful actions. For Jones, "contemplation is mysticism."[12]

> Mystical experience is consciousness of direct and imme-
> diate relationship with some transcendent reality, which,
> in the moment of experience, is believed to be God.[13]

Jones reminds us that by directly connecting with the truth of our divine beloved energy, we are cultivating love, compassion, and happiness in ourselves and in the world, and that this journey of awakening is one we are already engaged in and prepared for. In

11. Quoted in Steere, *Quaker Spirituality*, 10.
12. Jones, *Luminous Trail*, 19.
13. Jones, "Mystic's Experience of God," 638.

"Lighted Lives," a sermon preached at Trinity Church in Boston on Sunday, December 11, 1932, Jones claimed:

> The task of religion is not like that of laboriously endeavoring to teach an elephant to fly; it is rather the discovery of the potential capacities for flight in a being that is framed for the upper air.[14]

Jones' writings did much to interpret and apply historical Quaker and other Christian teachings to life in the United States. A politically active peacemaker, Jones became in 1917 one of the primary cofounders of the AFSC, an organization originally created to support conscientious objectors by providing them with an opportunity to serve those suffering during World War I, rather than to serve in the military. The AFSC expanded worldwide and has developed programs to help civilians during wars, as well as to alleviate famines in Russia, Europe, Asia, India, the Middle East, and Africa. In the United States, AFSC has been involved in working for justice and peace with Mexican Americans, Native Americans, migrant workers, prisoners, and the poor. Currently, AFSC is conducting the Wage Peace Campaign to end the U.S. war in Iraq.

Rufus Jones taught psychology, philosophy, ethics, and the development of Christian thought for over forty years at Haverford College in Pennsylvania. His ideas were precursors for Carl Rogers's developing his "positive psychology." Jones had a profound influence on many of his students, including Howard Thurman, who studied with Jones in 1929 and later became a minister, civil rights leader, and founder, in 1944, of San Francisco's Church for the Fellowship of All Peoples. Another student of Jones', Thomas Kelly, became an important figure in Quaker development in America.

Thomas Kelly

Thomas Kelly was born on June 4, 1893, on a farm in southwestern Ohio, where his parents had reopened an old Quaker meetinghouse. Kelly studied at Wilmington and Haverford Colleges and later came under the spell of Rufus Jones. Further experiences with Quaker life inspired him to take direct action during World War I. In 1917 and

14. Jones, "Lighted Lives," 148.

1918 Kelly volunteered to work with German prisoners of war in England. In 1919, he completed his bachelor of divinity degree at Hartford Seminary in Connecticut. Afterwards, he and his wife, Lael, worked for eighteen months with the AFSC in Berlin. Kelly received a PhD in philosophy from Hartford Theological Seminary. In 1925 he began teaching philosophy at Earlham College in Richmond, Indiana, but in the late 1930s left Indiana to serve as the director of the AFSC in Germany as Hitler and the Nazis were coming into power. After returning to the United States, Kelly often lectured on the integration of social change and spirituality, and wrote a number of theses, pamphlets, and books, including *Testament of Devotion*. He died in 1941, shortly before World War II began.

Direct and Personal Awareness of God's Presence

Quakers differ from many other Christians in part because of their complete commitment to and reliance upon the personal experiential awareness of the presence, love, and guidance of God in the Father, the Son, and the Holy Spirit. This simple and total reliance is the primary process or "liturgy" in most Quaker "meetings for worship," which are made up primarily of simple prayerful silences in which each person is encouraged to establish such awareness of Presence and communion with the Seed or Light as he or she is blessed to experience.

Quakers rely on personal awareness of the Holy One's guidance to inspire and inform their thoughts, words, and actions. Their non-violent work for peace is rooted in spiritual practice. Quakers see that the potential for awareness of the Divine—the kingdom of God—is within everyone and available to all. In Rufus Jones' words:

> Religion, on its upward-reaching side, is just joyous companionship with God.[15]

Thomas Kelly and Rufus Jones realized clearly the Divine One's presence in the human soul. They also realized the violent conditions of the world. Through their direct awareness of the presence and will of God, they discovered strength and inspiration, and touched upon deep and clear insights that served to motivate and guide their peacemaking. Their actions and writings continue to inspire Quakers

15. Fosdick, *Rufus Jones*, 255.

today in integrating personal freedom and collective social change. According to Thomas Kelly,

> The times are severe, the need is great, and we must hasten: we all agree. But whither shall we hasten? Two directions we must hasten, in order to plumb the depths and scale the heights of life. We must hasten unto God; and we must hasten into the world. But the first is the prime need; though the world be aflame by its own blindness and hate, and narrow ideals. We must first hasten unto God. Men whose heads have not rested in the bosom of God are not yet ready to be saviors of the world.[16]

Following the teachings of Jesus and of other great leaders in social change and spiritual liberation, Kelly, Jones, and other Quakers invite us to see God in others, and to treat all people—even a so-called enemy—as we would like to be treated. The lives of many Quakers have been devoted to transforming the violent interpersonal and international systems of reward and punishment into relationships based on gratitude and positive contribution. Rufus Jones sums up the Quaker point of view:

> Our war-shattered world cannot be rebuilt, our selfish and commercial age cannot be saved from its poor, thin self and prepared for service to others until the infinite worth and preciousness of men becomes the active spring and motive in the lives, both of capitalists and laborers, of church people and those of no church.[17]

Quakers cannot accept war and other violence because they see people literally and truly as children of God, created in God's image and capable of fellowship, communion, and union with God. War and violence desecrate our lives and prevent us from realizing or actualizing our human potential for being at peace with ourselves and with others. When fear, hatred, and other forms of violence live in us, they leave no room for love, empathy, or gratitude, and diminish the possibility for peace. Jones and Kelly both described the impulse to experience peace and joy as something larger than our own choice,

16. Kelly, *Eternal Promise*, 109–16.
17. Fosdick, *Rufus Jones*, 263–64.

but as a journey we are continually drawn into by a deeper source always seeking us and drawing us towards our true selves. Thomas Kelly says,

> To discover God is to come to know our true self.[18]

Rufus Jones and Thomas Kelly challenged all Christians and their churches to not be satisfied with religion as an activity limited to beliefs, ideas, and rituals, but to manifest love and compassion in their own lives, with peacemaking through nonviolent action based in the teachings of Jesus.

> If this experiment of ours of carrying love and service right into the areas of war and hate could be expanded, widened out to include for instance all the persons who belong to the Church of Christ, it would probably end war and make possible a new kind of world. [19]

> The church by its weakness and supine worldliness, shows desperate need of its radical reorientation, and fundamentally its rediscovery that religion is primarily built around God, joy in God, fellowship and love and victory and peace in God, not around the world; and that salvation is built, not upon forums for discussion of public affairs, but upon blood. By blood I mean not theological blood, but human-divine blood, yours and mine, poured out in self-forgetful consecration of God's renovation of a world in unspeakable need and suffering and darkness of vision.[20]

Relaxing Self-Cherishing and Expanding Selfless Service

Quakers, like many other Christians and practitioners of other religious or spiritual traditions understand that spiritual growth involves recognizing and then transforming an ego-based experience focused on self-cherishing to an attitude characterized by freedom, intercon-

18. Kelly, *Eternal Promise*, 123.
19. Fosdick, *Rufus Jones*, 269.
20. Kelly, *Eternal Promise*, 109–16.

nection, and selfless service. Quaker literature sometimes calls this aspect of spiritual growth "the great unselfing." On this matter, during his 1939 William Penn Lecture at the Arch Street Meeting House in Philadelphia, Thomas Kelly quoted the thirteenth-century Christian mystic Meister Eckhart: "'There are plenty to follow our Lord halfway, but not the other half. They will give up possessions, friends and honors, but it touches them too closely to disown themselves.'"[21]

More than anything else, our attachment to self separates us from God and from others. Selfishness—being unconsciously caught in our own desires and fears—must diminish in order for us to increase our awareness of God's presence and to cultivate peace. By opening to God and Truth, we connect with the life force infinitely greater and more powerful than the self. Through challenging self-cherishing and developing a commitment to serve others, we come to notice that we are deeply connected with all that is alive, and that our happiness is interconnected with the happiness of all beings. As the Dalai Lama has written, "Disregard your own well-being and cherish the well-being of others."[22] Kelly claims,

> In such a sense of Presence there is a vast background of cosmic Love and tender care for all things (plants included, I find for myself), but in the foreground arise special objects of love and concern, and tender responsibility.[23]

Rufus Jones wrote of the path of awakening to the power of love as manifesting through devotion to God, a commitment to serve others, and fellowship with Christ. Like the radiant energy and warmth of sunlight available to all, the power of unconditional love is also indiscriminate.

> It is not a hiding God; it is a self-revealing God . . . He is essentially Love—Agape . . . a unique type of Love, a Love that pours itself out regardless of merit, or desert—it floods out like the sun to reach the just and the

---

21. Kelly, "Holy Obedience," 26.

22. Dalai Lama XIV, *Training the Mind*, Verse 1. Accessed February 21, 2008. Online: http://www.dalailama.com/page.18.htm.

23. Kelly, *Testament of Devotion*, 100.

unjust. If we are looking for the Divine Yes, here it is, in all its splendor.[24]

Increasing an awareness of God's presence leads to awareness of the causes and conditions for happiness and the causes and conditions for suffering. The silence and consensus of Quaker meetings reveal clear and specific strategies that help cultivate peace in our own hearts, minds, and relationships. Freedom from common narcissistic concerns, fears, and desires creates room for us to take interest in addressing the suffering of others. Thomas Kelley describes the Quaker experience:

> Friends' or Quakers' experiences reveal over and over again that the personal awareness of the Presence, Light or God is totally satisfying. It is its own end and reason for being. However, awareness of the Presence of God also gives rise to "concerns" or "social concerns." Such "concerns," as Quakers call them, begin with people's awareness of the Holy One's leadings specifically for them. Quaker concerns arise from the Holy One within and among us motivating and guiding us personally— and often as congregations and other groups—to specific nonviolent work for peace and other helpful service. Quaker history is full of thousands of people who took great risks, made significant sacrifices and did much work because they felt themselves to be called, guided or inspired by the Holy One, the Seed or Light—and because they had the faith and fortitude to follow the Divine guidance they received.[25]

The spiritual approach to the nonviolent peacemaking of the Quakers resembles closely, or perhaps is identical with, Gandhi's. Gandhi said, "My own experience is that whenever I have acted non-violently I have been led to it and sustained in it by the higher prompting of an unseen power. Through my own will I should have miserably failed."[26] In 1927 Rufus Jones visited with Gandhi at his ashram and was impressed by the Indian leader's integration of spiritual practice and nonviolent social change.

24. Jones, *Luminous Trail*, 20.

25. Kelly, *Eternal Promise*, 26.

26. Gandhi, *Gandhi on Non-Violence*, 36.

The Quaker tradition is grounded in a strong commitment to two primary aspects of nonviolent peacemaking: 1) refusing to participate in, support, or cooperate with violence—often called resistance, noncooperation, civil disobedience, divine obedience or conscientious objection; and 2) working to facilitate the positive, constructive aspects of nonviolent peacemaking. Gandhi had described these two aspects of nonviolence as obstructive and constructive, with an emphasis on the second. Jones connects these ideas to Quaker practices:

> The Quaker flatly insists that [war] is absolutely and eternally wrong morally, that Christianity and war are utterly incompatible . . . This position goes back to and is grounded in the Quaker's idea of the nature of human personality, for this is the tap-root of all Quaker idealisms. There is something divine, something of God, in every person. The eternal passion of God, the whole redemptive story of the gospels, gets its significance in the tremendous fact that man and God belong together, are meant for each other and that beings like us are potential sons of God. To become a person, in the real sense of the word, is to awake to the consciousness of the divine relationship, to feel the inherent possibilities of sonship with God, to draw upon the inexhaustible supplies of grace, to enter into the actual inheritance of this divine-human privilege and to live in it and practice it. But this process of realizing the possibilities of life, this mighty business of becoming persons, can go on only in an atmosphere of human love and fellowship, and in an environment of cooperation.[27]

Rufus Jones and Thomas Kelly described the benefits of not turning away from suffering but meeting it with a compassionate and open heart. This nonresistance, or willingness to suffer in the name of love, has given Christians, Hindus, Buddhists, Jews, Muslims—people of all spiritual traditions—unlimited power to oppose violence, and infinite strength to create peace. In this realm George Fox's civil disobedience and willingness to go to jail rather than give up his faith provides a role model for American Quakers. He was arrested eight times and spent a total of eight years in prison.

27. Fosdick, *Rufus Jones*, 271–72.

Formerly the world spread itself out before us, focused about ourselves. We were the center . . . now we must say it is given to us to see the world's suffering, throughout, and bear it, Godlike, upon our shoulders, and suffer with all things and all men, and rejoice with all things and all men, and we see the hills clap their hands for joy, and we clap our hands with them.[28]

Entrance Into Suffering: Birth of Compassion

Another fruit of holy obedience is entrance into suffering. I would not magnify joy and rapture, although they are un-speakably great in the committed life. For joy and rapture need no advocates. But we shrink from suffering and can easily call all suffering an evil thing . . . I recently had an unforgettable hour with a Hindu monk. He knew the se-cret of this paradox which we discussed together: "Nothing matters; everything matters." It is a key of entrance into suffering. He who knows only one-half of the paradox can never enter the door of mystery and survive.[29]

Thomas Kelly gave his "Holy Obedience" speech after returning from a trip to Europe, where he witnessed firsthand the devastation of Fascism as World War II began to develop. Kelly advocated simplic-ity and devotion, appealing to his audience to give up busyness, even the busyness that can come with what we may think of as a "spiritual path." He pointed out that the benefit of a simplified life is radiant joy, and that the development of compassion requires openness to suffering rather than automatic aversion to it.

There is a lusty, adolescent way of thought among us which oversimplifies the question of suffering. It merely says, "Let us remove it." . . . The heart is stretched through suffering, and enlarged.[30]

---

28. Kelly, *Eternal Promise*, 27.
29. Kelly, "Holy Obedience," 39–40.
30. Ibid., 41, 43.

An awakening to God is also an awakening to the world, to its joy and its pain. Kelly pointed to the benefits of greeting the suffering with the compassion and love of Christ, instead of trying to escape from it.

> The beyond which is within opens up yet another beyond, the world of earthly need and pain and joy and beauty. For the Inner Light illumines not only God, but the world. Its discovery within ourselves does not insulate us, together with the Eternal, in solitary ecstasy, away from the poverties of earth; it opens our yes to the old world and shows it to us in a new way.[31]

Thomas Kelly discovered the presence and reality of God through personal experience and an "opening," preceded by a period of substantial personal struggle. He said that the Spirit or Seed guides and directs us, sometimes with awesome and inescapable power, and sometimes with the gentle softness of the lightest breeze.

> Greater intelligence in the direction of human affairs is no sufficient ground of hope, if the motivations of the heart are not transformed. . . . We are men of double personalities. We have slumbering demons within us. We all have also a dimly-formed Christ within us. We've been too ready to say that the demonic man within us is the natural and the real man, and the Christ-man within us is the unnatural and the unreal self. But the case is that our surface potentialities are for selfishness and greed, for tooth and claw. But deep within, in the whispers of the heart, is the surging call of the Eternal Christ, hidden within us all. By an inner isthmus we are connected with the mainland of the Eternal Love. Surface living has brought on the world's tragedy. Deeper living leads us to the Eternal Christ, hidden in us all. Absolute loyalty to this inner Christ is the only hope of a new humanity.[32]

Kelly pointed out that suffering is not always beneficial or easy. He realized that to be able to accept, embrace, and transform suffer-

---

31. Kelly, *Eternal Promise*, 26–27.
32. Ibid., 40–41.

ing as Jesus had, requires development of the soul force and personal cultivation of the seed of love within.

> There is nothing automatic about suffering, so that suffering infallibly produces great souls . . . No, there is nothing about suffering such that it automatically purges the dross from human nature and brings heroic souls upon the scene. Suffering can blast and blight an earnest but unprepared soul, and damn it utterly to despair. No, only those who go into the travail of today, bearing a seed within them, a seed of awareness of the heavenly dimensions of humanity, can return in joy.[33]

Rufus Jones and Thomas Kelly referred to the presence of the love of Jesus with the image of a seed growing and developing through compassion for the suffering of others. In being mindful and present with others as they suffer, we bring Christ to life in our thoughts and actions. According to Kelly,

> In each of us the amazing and dangerous seed of Christ is present. It is only a seed. It is very small, like the grain of mustard seed. The Christ that is formed in us is small indeed, but He is great with eternity. But if we dare to take this awakened seed of Christ into the midst of the world's suffering, it will grow. That's why the Quaker work camps are important. Take a young man or a young woman in whom Christ is only dimly formed, but one in whom the seed of Christ is alive. Put him into a distressed area, into a refugee camp, into a poverty region. Let him go into the world's suffering, bearing this seed with him, and in suffering it will grow, and Christ will be more and more fully formed in him. As the grain of mustard seed grew so large that the birds found shelter in it, so the man who bears an awakened seed into the world's suffering will grow until he becomes a refuge for many.[34]

In our present age, when war and weapons development may contribute to a planetary omnicide, compassion is part of the Christian challenge and responsibility. Compassion is a fruit of our

33. Kelly, *Eternal Promise*, 41.
34. Ibid., 41–44.

grace and of awareness of the awakened seed of Christ within and among us. Compassion enables and motivates us to act in ways that help those in need. The awareness of our own potential for peace is present in relative proportion to our willingness to surrender our narrowly selfish interests in order to help people who are in greater need then we. The more that we see peace in ourselves, the more we see it in others. The more that we act for peace as Jesus taught, the more peace and happiness we will know in our own heart, mind, and life, even when our work necessitates accepting suffering without desiring retaliation.

We are all called to live in love, peace, and understanding with our neighbors, and to work for relational, social, and international processes that facilitate peace and social justice, so that all people have opportunities to experience the great joy and peace of knowing God. This Quaker way to peacemaking is the Christian way to peacemaking. It is a path of peace that is not waiting for a messiah or leader to change the world but is itself a catalyst for change in our world.

> No religious dictators will save the world; no giant figure of heroic size will stalk across the stage of history today, as a new Messiah. But in simple, humble imperfect men like you and me wells up the spring of hope. We have this treasure of the seed in earthen vessels—very earthen vessels. You and I know how imperfect we are. And yet those little demonstrations of love and goodwill, such as the feeding of children in Spain, the direction of transit stations for refugees in Holland and Cuba, the reconstruction of lives in the coal fields, are being carried on by just such earthen vessels. These tasks shine like tiny candles in the darkness—deeds done in the midst of suffering, through which shines the light of the Living Christ, deeds that stir hope that humanity as a whole will be aroused to yield to the press and surge of the Eternal Love within them.[35]

35. Kelly, *Eternal Promise*, 41–44.

4

Martin Luther King Jr.

MOST AMERICANS and many from other nations regard the Reverend Dr. Martin Luther King Jr. as one of the great leaders of the civil rights movement in the United States. His compassion-based work to end racism, classism, and segregation through nonviolent direct action continues to influence contemporary social-change activists worldwide. King's life serves as an example of the potential of peacemaking that combines religious and spiritual practice with principled, persistent methods of nonviolent political action. The patient dedication of this third-generation Baptist pastor to creating "beloved community" has inspired thousands to resist injustice, positively influencing their lives. In his acceptance speech for the 1964 Nobel Peace Prize, King said, "Civilization and violence are antithetical concepts. . . . Nonviolence is the answer to the crucial political and moral question of our time."[1]

Rev. King's commitment to nonviolence was forged during the U.S. civil rights movement of the 1950s and '60s. In his February 28, 1954, sermon, "Rediscovering Lost Values," King told the congregation at Detroit's Second Baptist Church: "The great problem facing modern man is that the means *by* which we live have outdistanced the spiritual ends *for* which we live," reminding them, "you shall reap what you sow."[2]

His commitment to nonviolent "Christianity in action" gained wider recognition a year later with his leadership of the 382-day bus boycott in Montgomery, Alabama, where King followed the lead of Rosa Parks, an African American woman who had refused to give up her seat to a white person.

1. King, "Nobel Prize," 224–25.
2. See King, *Strength to Love*, 76.

At that time, African American people in much of the South were segregated from white Americans in their use of public buses, bathrooms, drinking fountains, and seats in restaurants. Access to jobs, healthcare, education, voting, and fair judicial treatment were also restricted. The racial prejudice of the time remained as a residual cultural imprint from the violent legacy of 244 years of slavery in America from 1619 to 1863.

As a result of Martin Luther King's work and the efforts of many individuals and organizations such as the National Association for the Advancement of Colored People (NAACP), the Congress of Racial Equality, the Student Nonviolent Coordinating Committee (SNCC), and the Southern Christian Leadership Conference (SCLC), the Civil Rights Act passed in 1964, and the Voting Rights Act in 1965, securing for African Americans rights to all privileges of the United States constitution.

Martin Luther King Jr. and Jesus: Nonviolence Is Key

Rev. King drew upon the life and teachings of Jesus to develop an understanding of, and language for, nonviolent resistance in the United States. King interpreted the words and actions of Jesus as a direct challenge to the dominant structures of violence. King found in the career of Jesus a warrant to explore the human capacity for individual and collective goodness in order to transform society, a capacity based in the conscious development of compassion, loving kindness, and forgiveness.

> I think this is what Jesus meant when he said, "I come not to bring peace but a sword." Now Jesus didn't mean he came to start war, to bring a physical sword, and he didn't mean, I come not to bring positive peace. But I think what Jesus was saying in substance was this, that I come not to bring an old negative peace, which makes for stagnant passivity and deadening complacency, I come to bring something different, and whenever I come, a conflict is precipitated, between the old and the new,

whenever I come a struggle takes place between justice and injustice, . . . which is the Kingdom of God.[3]

For King, Jesus epitomized the nonviolent peacemaker who exemplified a life devoted to serving others: the heart of nonviolent peacemaking. He viewed Jesus as having been a dynamic preacher and outspoken leader in social change, who became targeted as a troublemaker and eventually was executed for his efforts to teach compassionate action.

> I know a man and I just want to talk about him a minute and maybe you will discover who I'm talking about as I go down the way, because he was a great one. And he just went about serving. He was born in an obscure village, the child of a poor peasant woman. And then he grew up in still another obscure village, where he worked as a carpenter until he was thirty years old. Then for three years, he just got on his feet and he was an itinerant preacher. And then he went about doing some things. He didn't have much. He never wrote a book. He never held an office. He never had a family. He never owned a house. He never went to college. He never visited a big city. He never went two hundred miles from where he was born. He did none of the usual things that the world would associate with greatness. He had no credentials but himself.
>
> He was thirty-three when the tide of public opinion turned against him. They called him a rabble-rouser. They called him a troublemaker. They said he was an agitator. He practiced civil disobedience; he broke injunctions. And so he was turned over to his enemies and went through the mockery of a trial. And the irony of it all is that his friends turned him over to them. One of his closest friends denied him. Another of his friends turned him over to his enemies. And while he was dying, the people who killed him gambled for his clothing, the only possession that he had in the world. When he was dead, he was buried in a borrowed tomb, through the pity of a friend.
>
> Nineteen centuries have come and gone and today, he stands as the most influential figure that ever entered human history. All of the armies that ever marched, all the

3. King, "Love, Law, and Civil Disobedience," 51.

navies that ever sailed, all the parliaments that ever sat, and all the kings that ever reigned put together have not affected the life of man on this earth as much as that one solitary life. His name may be a familiar one. But today I can hear them talking about him. Every now and then somebody says, "He's king of kings." And again I can hear somebody saying, "He's lord of lords." Somewhere else I can hear somebody saying, "In Christ there is no east nor west." And they go on and talk about . . . "In him there's no north and south, but one great fellowship of love throughout the whole wide world." He didn't have anything. He just went around serving and doing good. You can be on his right hand and his left hand if you serve. It's the only way in.[4]

Martin Luther King Jr. and Gandhi

Martin Luther King Jr. recognized Mohandas K. Gandhi as the man who popularized nonviolence in the twentieth century and as a great teacher of the power and universality of love and compassion, the roots of all religious traditions. Though King never met the mahatma before Gandhi's assassination in 1948, other civil rights leaders who had the opportunity to study with Gandhi and his disciples in India in the 1930s, '40s and '50s taught King the lessons and methods of the Indian leader's *Satyagraha* ("soul force" or "truth") movement.

From 1935 to 1936, Baptist minister Howard Thurman led a delegation of African Americans to meet with Gandhi. The Indian leader asked them to recognize that faith and religion in the United States had been abused to support racism. Gandhi challenged African Americans to explore the possibilities of Christianity invigorated with nonviolence and compassion. Thurman shared his new knowledge with King, and they adapted Gandhi's *Satyagraha* to the civil rights movement in North America.

> Nonviolent resistance had emerged as the technique of the civil rights movement, while love stood as the regulating ideal. In other words, Christ furnished the spirit and motivation, while Gandhi furnished the method.[5]

4. King, "Drum Major Instinct," 266.
5. King, "Experiment in Love," 17.

King adapted the Indian leader's method of combining spiritual practice with nonviolent direct action for use in the movement for civil rights in the United States. In 1959, King made a pilgrimage to the land where Gandhi had struggled for independence and peace. The journey confirmed and strengthened King's belief in nonviolence as the best tool for finding freedom.

> The trip [to India] had a great impact upon me personally. It was wonderful to be in Gandhi's land, to talk with his son, his grandsons, his cousins and other relatives: to share the reminiscences of his close comrades, to visit his ashrama, to see the countless memorials for him and finally to lay a wreath on his entombed ashes at Rajghat. I left India more convinced than ever before that nonviolent resistance is the most potent weapon available to oppressed people in their struggle for freedom.[6]

From Gandhi's example, King learned to use nonviolence not because of fear or lack of access to the tools of violent means, but because nonviolence was a more skillful method for achieving the goal of peace.

> If one uses this method because he is afraid or merely because he lacks the instruments of violence, he is not truly nonviolent. This is why Gandhi often said that if cowardice is the only alternative to violence, it is better to fight. He made this statement conscious of the fact that there is always another alternative; no individual or group need submit to any wrong, nor need they use violence to right that wrong; there is the way of nonviolent resistance.[7]

Peace Begins With the Self

Jesus taught that "the kingdom of God is within you" (Luke 17:21) and that peace begins with oneself. Martin Luther King Jr. developed compassion and the capacity to endure suffering in order to bring peace to himself and others. Recognizing and consciously diminishing our inner greed, anger, and fear enables us to cultivate and share

6. King, "My Trip to the Land of Gandhi," 25.
7. King, "Experiment in Love," 17.

compassion, love, and peace. Reducing our habits of violent thinking and action creates peace within the self and peace between people.

> True nonviolent resistance is not unrealistic submission to evil power. It is rather a courageous confrontation of evil by the power of love, in the faith that it is better to be the recipient of violence than the inflictor of it, since the latter only multiplies the existence of violence and bitterness in the universe, while the former may develop a sense of shame in the opponent and thereby bring about a transformation and change of heart. Nonviolent resistance does call for love, but it is not a sentimental love. It is a very stern love that would organize itself into collective action to right a wrong by taking on itself suffering.[8]

Nonviolence Is the Active Power of Love

Like Jesus, King and Gandhi recognized that nonviolence is much more than the absence of violence, and that peace is much more than the absence of war. These great teachers embraced their friends *and* enemies as self, returning love in the face of oppression and hatred.

> I still believe that love is the most durable power in the world. Love stands at the center of the cosmos. As John says, "God is love." He who loves is a participant in the being of God. He who hates does not know God.[9]

"The Sanskrit word *ahimsa*, sometimes is translated as "passive resistance," leading to the misinterpretation that nonviolence is inactive or weak. Gandhi's *ahimsa* and Jesus' *agape* describe the *active* power of love within each of us that can be used to bring out the same in others.

> *Agape* is not a weak, passive love. It is love in action. *Agape* is love seeking to preserve and create community. It is insistence on community even when one seeks to break it. It is a willingness to go to any length to restore community. It doesn't stop at the first mile, but it goes the second mile to restore community. It is a willingness

8. King, "My Trip to the Land of Gandhi," 26.
9. King, "Most Durable Power," 11.

to forgive, not seven times, but seventy times seven to restore community. The cross is the eternal expression of the length to which God will go in order to restore broken community. The resurrection is a symbol of God's triumph over all the forces that seek to block community. The Holy Spirit is the continuing community creating reality that moves through history. Booker T. Washington was right: "Let no man pull you so low as to make you hate him." When he pulls you that low he brings you to the point of defying creation, and thereby becoming depersonalized.[10]

Nonviolence seeks to reduce and eliminate the seeds of violence that manifest themselves in thoughts, feelings, and actions. Peace grows from gratitude for life and from love for other living beings, not from the temporary results of violence or silent complicity.

True peace is not merely the absence of some negative force—tension, confusion or war; it is the presence of some positive force—justice, good will and brotherhood.[11]

To extend this love even to those who hate you is the farthest limit of ahimsa (nonviolence). It pushes at the boundaries of consciousness itself.[12]

Recognizing the interconnectedness of all life, King brought the Christian teaching of "do to others as you would have them do to you" to the civil rights struggle of the United States. In his April 16, 1963, "Letter From Birmingham City Jail," King wrote, "All life is interrelated," and, "We are caught in an inescapable network of mutuality, tied in a single garment of destiny."[13]

In the final analysis, *agape* means a recognition of the fact that all life is interrelated. All humanity is involved in a single process and all men are brothers. To the degree that I harm my brother, no matter what he is doing to me, to that extent I am harming myself. For example, white men often refuse federal aid to education in order

10. King, "Experiment in Love," 20.
11. King, "Nonviolence and Racial Justice," 6.
12. Easwaran, *Gandhi, the Man*, 89.
13. King, "Letter," 290.

to avoid giving the Negro his rights; but because all men are brothers they cannot deny Negro children without harming their own. They end, all efforts to the contrary, by hurting themselves. Why is this? Because men are brothers. If you harm me, you harm yourself.[14]

Loving our enemy in the midst of conflict requires deep spiritual and psychological practice and growth. In moments of anger or pain, it requires vigilant awareness and patience to return to love. You can practice nonviolence every day, at home or at work, whether or not you are ever involved in a wider social struggle. In fact, relationships with family and friends can be wonderful places to practice the nonviolence and love that Rev. King taught. As great as the obstacles to love are, the potentials and benefits of love are much greater. This kind of love is the furthest thing from unrealistic or sentimental idealism or from the denial of the realities of suffering and injustice. The centrality of love in both nonviolent peacemaking and Christianity reveals the deep connection of these traditions, both of which emphasize that love and compassion unlock the door to ultimate reality and boundless joy.

> *Agape.* . . . is an overflowing love which is purely spontaneous, unmotivated, groundless and creative. It is not set in motion by any quality or function of its object. It is the love of God operating in the human heart.[15]

Compassion over Coercion

Martin Luther King Jr. rejected force, coercion, humiliation, or the threat of punishment as methods for social change. Instead he explored the alternative of compassionate action as a method for transforming one's enemies rather than defeating them.

> A second point is that nonviolent resistance does not seek to defeat or humiliate the opponent, but to win his friendship and understanding. The nonviolent resister must often express his protest through noncooperation or boycotts, but he realizes that non-cooperation and

14. King, "Experiment in Love," 20.
15. Ibid., 19.

boycotts are not ends themselves, they are merely means to awaken a sense of moral shame in the opponent. The end is redemption and reconciliation. The aftermath of nonviolence is the creation of the beloved community, while the aftermath of violence is tragic bitterness.[16]

King knew that violence only fueled hate, anger, and fear, and that the antidotes to these causes of suffering were compassion and love. He was dedicated to developing a strategy—"Christianity in action"—to replace the failed method of making war in order to end war and practicing violence to end violence.

Hate begets hate; violence begets violence; toughness begets a greater toughness. We must meet the forces of hate with the power of love; we must meet physical force with soul force. Our aim must never be to defeat or humiliate the white man, but to win his friendship and understanding.[17]

Defeat Injustice, Not People

Nonviolence directs its resistance against the conditioned ways of thinking and acting prevalent among human beings and at the violent social systems and structures that cause suffering and that perpetuate racism, war, and poverty. Rev. King advocated labor strikes, sit-ins, marches, boycotts, rallies, and civil disobedience because they could transform both the nonviolent practitioner as well as the opponent. King said, nonviolence seeks to defeat injustice, not people. Nonviolence chooses love instead of hate.[18]

A third characteristic of this method is that the attack is directed against forces of evil rather than against persons who are caught in those forces. It is evil we are seeking to defeat, not the persons victimized by evil. Those of us who struggle against racial injustice must come to see

16. King, "Nonviolence and Racial Justice," 7–8.

17. King, *Stride Toward Freedom*, 449, in *A Testament of Hope*.

18. Cf. King, "Power of Nonviolence," 12–13: "the nonviolent resister seeks to attack the evil system rather than the individuals who happen to be caught up in the system . . . at the center of our movement stood the philosophy of love."

> that the basic tension is not between races . . . The tension
> is at bottom between justice and injustice, between the
> forces of light and the forces of darkness. And if there is
> a victory it will be a victory not merely for fifty thousand
> Negroes, but a victory for justice and the forces of light.
> We are out to defeat injustice and not white persons who
> may happen to be unjust.[19]

Nonviolence demands compassion for those who cause suffering. On the cross, Jesus provides the greatest example of this capacity for forgiveness: "Father, forgive them, for they know not what they are doing" (Luke 23:34). All religious traditions teach that every human being is capable of compassion and that the language and systems of domination have separated us from our capacity to love. These systems are what needs to be defeated, not the individual beings subjugated to those systems.

> One seeks to defeat the unjust system, rather than individuals who are caught in that system. The nonviolent resister seeks to attack the evil system rather than individuals who happen to be caught up in the system.[20]

Peace Is the Path: Means and Ends

Gandhi wrote, "The means may be likened to a seed, the end to a tree; and there is just the same inviolable connection between the means and the end as there is between the seed and the tree."[21] King emphasized that the civil rights movement was "based on the philosophy that ends and means must cohere" and that "in the long run, we must see that the end is pre-existent in the means."[22]

> If we are to have peace in the world, men and nations must
> embrace the nonviolent affirmation that ends and means
> must cohere . . . We must pursue peaceful ends through
> peaceful means . . . We will never have peace in the world

19. King, "Nonviolence and Racial Justice," 8.

20. King, "Love, Law and Civil Disobedience," 47.

21. Gandhi, *All Men Are Brothers*, 75.

22. King, "Love, Law and Civil Disobedience," 45; "Address Before the National Press Club," 102.

until men everywhere recognize that ends are not cut off from means, because the means represent the ideal in the making and the end in process and ultimately you can't reach good ends through evil means, because the means represent the seed and the end represents the tree.[23]

Resist Not Evil: Suffer Without Retaliation

Nonviolent peacemaking depends upon the principle of suffering without retaliation. Jesus willingly suffered humiliations, insults, a violent beating, and crucifixion without retaliation in word, gesture, or spirit. Martin Luther King Jr. applied this teaching to the civil rights struggle when he and many others faced the violence of bombings, police riots, attack dogs, water hoses and imprisonment.

> A sixth point that characterizes nonviolent resistance is a willingness to accept suffering without retaliation, to accept blows from the opponent without striking back. "Rivers of blood may have to flow before we gain our freedom, but it must be our blood," Gandhi said to his countrymen. The nonviolent resister is willing to accept violence if necessary, but never to inflict it. He does not seek to dodge jail. If going to jail is necessary, he enters it "as a bridegroom enters the bride's chamber."[24]

Jesus' teaching of "resist not evil" offers an alternative, loving response to violence and evil: one that calls for understanding and compassion rather than for brute force and retaliation. King, Gandhi, and Jesus all were killed by people who opposed their teachings of "turn the other cheek" and the redemptive power of unearned suffering.

> One may well ask, "What is the nonviolent resister's justification for this ordeal to which he invites men, for this mass political application of the ancient doctrine of turning the other cheek?" The answer is found in the realization that unearned suffering is redemptive. Suffering, the nonviolent resister realizes, has tremendous educational and transforming possibilities. "Things of fundamental

23. King, "Christmas Sermon," 254–55.
24. King, "Experiment in Love," 18.

importance to people are not secured by reason alone, but have to be purchased with their suffering," said Gandhi. He continues: "Suffering is infinitely more powerful than the law of the jungle for converting the opponent and opening his ears which are otherwise shut to the voice of reason."[25]

King realized the dangers and sacrifice that he faced as he stood up for truth and justice. He and his family faced continual death threats, and in 1956 their home in Montgomery, Alabama, was bombed. In 1958 while promoting his first book *Stride Toward Freedom*, King was stabbed.

> Honesty impels me to admit that such a stand will require willingness to suffer and sacrifice, so don't despair if you are condemned and persecuted for righteousness' sake. Whenever you take a stand for truth and justice, you are liable to scorn. Often you will be called an impractical idealist or a dangerous radical. Sometimes it might mean going to jail. If such is the case you must honorably grace the jail with your presence. It might even mean physical death. But if physical death is the price that some must pay to free their children from a permanent life of psychological death, then nothing could be more Christian.[26]

Truth Is Central

Gandhi named his nonviolent social change movement *Satyagraha*, meaning "truth force" or "soul force." To Gandhi, as to the Apostle John and many other spiritual teachers, truth is God and God is truth (see John 3:33). For Gandhi and for Martin Luther King, standing up for the truth was central to appreciating life and making peace.

> I still believe that standing up for the truth of God is the greatest thing in the world. This is the end of life. The end of life is not to be happy. The end of life is not to

25. King, "Experiment in Love," 18.
26. King, "Most Durable Power," 9.

achieve pleasure and avoid pain. The end of life is to do that will of God, come what may.[27]

King often referred to nonviolent peacemaking as "soul force" because its goal and method grows from what is sacred in the human soul. Truth means seeing the reality of the world as it is, not as we suppose it to be or wish it to be. The interconnection and interdependence between living beings is the central truth of life and is a core tenet of all spiritual and religious traditions

> We are challenged to develop a world perspective. No individual can live alone, no nation can live alone and anyone who feels that he can live alone is sleeping through a revolution. The world in which we live is geographically one. The challenge that we face today is to make it one in terms of brotherhood. . . . Through our scientific and technological genius, we have made of this world a neighborhood and yet . . . we have not had the ethical commitment to make of it a brotherhood. But somehow and in some way, we have got to do this. We must all learn to live together as brothers. Or we will all perish together as fools. We are tied together in the single garment of destiny, caught in an inescapable network of mutuality. And whatever affects one directly affects all indirectly. . . . This is the way God's universe is made; this is the way it is structured.[28]

Spiritual and Psychological Growth of Practitioners

Martin Luther King Jr. believed that every human being has the potential for peace, a growth potential he called "the image of God." Quakers call it "the Seed," and Buddhists refer to it as "Buddha Nature." King acknowledged that the first to benefit from nonviolence is the one committed to compassionate action.

> The nonviolent approach does not immediately change the heart of the oppressor. It first does something to the hearts and souls of those committed to it. It gives

27. Ibid., 9.

28. King, "Remaining Awake," 269.

them new self-respect; it calls up resources of strength and courage that they did not know they had. Finally it reaches the opponent and so stirs his conscience that reconciliation becomes a reality.[29]

King believed that developing the spiritual and psychological attention and growth that nonviolence requires would allow people to forsake the selfish hunt for pleasure, enabling them to suffer without the desire to retaliate. King witnessed the power of nonviolence to transform people, empowering them with courage and freedom.

> Another of the major strengths of the nonviolent weapon is its strange power to transform and transmute the individuals who subordinate themselves to its disciplines, investing them with a cause that is larger than themselves. They become, for the first time, somebody; and they have, for the first time, the courage to be free. When the Negro finds the courage to be free, he faces dogs and guns and clubs and fire hoses totally unafraid, and the white men with those dogs, guns, clubs and fire hoses see that the Negro they have traditionally called "boy" has become a man.[30]

The principal characteristics of King's revolution of consciousness included increased empathy, understanding and compassion, and decreased judgment and condemnation of others. Following Jesus, King and Gandhi sought to reduce their own self-interest and increase their service to others.

> There comes a time when an individual becomes irresistible and his action become all-pervasive in its effect. This comes when he reduces himself to zero.[31]

To change society as Gandhi and King wished required ongoing development of their own internal spiritual and psychological experiences. They practiced acts of compassion and wisdom, the heart of a truly nonviolent revolution.

---

29. King, *Stride Toward Freedom*, in *A Testament of Hope*, 486–87.
30. King, "*Playboy* Interview," 349.
31. Gandhi, quoted in Easwaran, *Gandhi, the Man*, 150.

Violence, even in self-defense, creates more problems than it solves. Only a refusal to hate or kill can put an end to the chain of violence in the world and lead us toward a community where men can live together without fear. Our goal is to create a beloved community and this will require a qualitative change in our souls as well as a quantitative change in our lives.[32]

Nonviolence: Necessary for Survival

In his Nobel Peace Prize acceptance speech, King put the matter quite simply for our nuclear age: "Civilization and violence are antithetical concepts."[33] We no longer have the luxury of imagining theoretical ways of stopping a way of life that is at war with life, a war that threatens our very existence.

> It is no longer a choice, my friends, between violence and nonviolence. It is either nonviolence or nonexistence, and the alternative to disarmament, the alternative to a greater suspension of nuclear tests, the alternative to strengthening the United Nations and thereby disarming the whole world may well be a civilization plunged into the abyss of annihilation, and our earthly habitat would be transformed into an inferno that even the mind of Dante could not imagine.[34]

King sensed the urgency of modern environmental, political, and social crises. He believed that we no longer have the luxury of simply talking about the violence and suffering. We live in a time when we must take action against the causes of war, poverty, and racism. King taught that unity and love would bring real freedom.

> In a world facing the revolt of ragged and hungry masses of God's children; in a world torn between the tensions of East and West, white and colored, individualists and collectivists; in a world whose cultural and spiritual power lags so far behind her technological capabilities that we

32. King, "Nonviolence: The Only Road to Freedom," 57–58.
33. King, "Nobel Prize," 224.
34. King, "Remaining Awake," 276.

live each day on the verge of nuclear co-annihilation; in this world, nonviolence is no longer an option for intellectual analysis, it is an imperative for action.[35]

King opposed the war in Vietnam and was beginning to merge the antiwar movement with the civil rights movement, linking poverty and violence. He criticized the U.S. government's choice to fund military research and action rather than peace and education, and was planning national economic boycotts, a massive march of the poor on Washington DC, and nonviolent city-wide "camp-ins."

> A nation that continues year after year to spend more money on military defense than on programs of social uplift is approaching spiritual death. America, the richest and most powerful nation in the world, can well lead the way in this revolution of values. There is nothing, except a tragic death wish to prevent us from reordering our priorities so that the pursuit of peace will take precedence over the pursuit of war. There is nothing to keep us from molding a recalcitrant status quo with bruised hands until we have fashioned it into a brotherhood.[36]

On April 3, 1968, Martin Luther King Jr. was in Memphis to push for improved pay and conditions for the city's sanitation workers. In what would be the last speech of his life, he declared, "I've been to the mountaintop and I've seen the promised land. I may not get there with you. But I want you to know, that we, as a people, will get to the promised land."[37] The following day he was assassinated.

Between 1957 and 1968, Martin Luther King Jr. wrote five books, traveled over six million miles, and held over 2500 public talks, bringing the struggle for justice and peace wherever he went. He carried the gospel of freedom in the struggles for integration, education, voting rights, economic opportunity, racial equality, and world peace. He continues to be a guiding force in the compassion-based movements for peace and justice in the world.

35. King, "Trumpet of Conscience," 653.

36. King, "Time to Break Silence," 241.

37. King, "I See the Promised Land," 286.

5

Dorothy Day and the *Catholic Worker*

DOROTHY DAY, a leader in the movement for peace and justice from the 1930s until 1980, continues to influence peacemakers worldwide. She brought the teachings of Jesus to life through nonviolent direct action and journalism. She nourished her efforts through practicing prayer, cultivating compassion, embracing poverty, and creating community. She integrated social change and spirituality into her daily life, combining political analysis and deep wisdom about how to address the modern crises of poverty, hunger, and war with compassionate actions based in the teachings of Jesus. Some recognize Dorothy Day as a "radical" activist; others consider her a saint. Really, she is both. In fact, the late Cardinal John O'Connor wrote vouching for her canonization in a letter to the Vatican in 2000.[1] The story of her life serves to remind us of the power of faith in Christ and adherence to nonviolence.

Dorothy Day was born on November 8, 1897, in Brooklyn. Dorothy's father, John Day, a sports writer and editor, disapproved of her radical politics. Her mother, Grace, much beloved by her children, raised Dorothy and her three brothers and one sister. The family moved to San Francisco but following the 1906 earthquake, relocated to Chicago's south side. Dorothy graduated from high school at the age of sixteen and attended the University of Illinois in Urbana for two years before she decided to move to New York to work as a reporter for the *Call*, a socialist daily newspaper. Later she wrote for other radical magazines and newspapers, including *The Masses, Commonweal,* and *America*. In 1932, she and Peter Maurin produced the first issue of their own newspaper, the *Catholic Worker.* By 1936 the *Catholic Worker*

---

1. http://www.catholicworker.org/dorothyday/canonizationtext.cfm? Number =82. Accessed February 20, 2008.

had become a national movement of houses of hospitality, providing food and shelter to the hungry and homeless.

Day participated in antiwar rallies and direct actions for civil and women's rights even though her acts of conscience often got her arrested and jailed. The last time she was jailed—in 1973, at age 76—she was on a picket line supporting César Chavez and California farm workers. Dorothy Day died on November 29, 1980.

Political Writing and Direct Action

An eager young reader, Dorothy Day was influenced by "class-conscious" writers of the early twentieth century who addressed injustice, violence, and poverty. *The Jungle*, by Upton Sinclair, and Jack London's books made a deep impression on her. She read anarchist authors such as Peter Kropotkin and Leo Tolstoy, and explored the political theories of Marx's economic determinism, as well as Communism and the socialism of Eugene Debs. In his introduction to Day's autobiography, *The Long Loneliness*, Catholic activist Daniel Berrigan wrote, "She was studying everything from the anarchist history of America to the New Testament."[2] Though Dorothy's work echoed the Communist call for workers of the world to unite, and though she sympathized with the socialist analysis of the economic causes and conditions for poverty and inequity, she disagreed with the violent tactics and antireligious sentiment that often accompanied these philosophies and movements. After she discovered that spirituality could nourish her political writing and activism, she converted to Catholicism, much to the dismay of other radical activists, including her husband.

Like Martin Luther King Jr., Day saw a link between the military aggression of the United States government and the struggles of the working class at home. She demonstrated against war in all its forms, and developed soup kitchens and houses of hospitality for the poor and homeless. She organized and participated in nonviolent direct actions against the Spanish-American War, World Wars I and II, and the wars in Korea and Vietnam—and she encouraged soldiers to refuse combat through conscientious objection. Day was among the first U.S. activists to recognize the rise of Nazism in Europe, and

2. Berrigan, "Introduction," ix.

believed that the American intention for entering the Second World War was to retain political and economic power, and not to save the Jews, as was popularly thought.

After dropping out of college, Day moved to New York where she got a job as a reporter for the *Call*, New York's socialist daily. Next she worked for the *Masses*, a magazine that opposed U.S. involvement in the First World War. The post office rescinded the mailing permit for the *Masses*, and later five editors of the paper were arrested and charged with sedition. Day's participation in protests, rallies, strikes, and demonstrations for peace, worker's rights, and women's suffrage led to her frequent arrest; the first arrest came in 1917 for her protesting at the White House against the exclusion of women as voters in elections. Police mistreated forty female protesters who responded with a hunger strike and were then freed by presidential order. Day's main desire was to contribute to the well-being of others; so in 1918, during the First World War, Day decided that being a journalist was not enough, and she began to study nursing in Brooklyn.

In 1932 Day traveled to Washington DC to report on the Communist Hunger March for *Commonweal* and *America* magazines. Protesters carried signs calling for jobs, healthcare, housing, unemployment insurance, social security, and aid for mothers and children. Though Day agreed with the social-change programs advocated by the marchers, she disagreed with the Communist organizers of the protest, who paid no attention to the spiritual component of revolutionary change.

After the Hunger March, Day struggled to find a personal way to integrate social change and spiritual growth. She went to the Shrine of the Immaculate Conception and prayed for clarity about how she could serve others.

> I offered up a special prayer, a prayer which came with tears and anguish, that some way would open up for me to use what talents I possessed for my fellow workers, for the poor.[3]

The very next day, it seemed that her prayer was answered. A French immigrant named Peter Maurin, a former Christian Brother now living a life of voluntary poverty, simplicity, prayer, and direct

3. Day, *Long Loneliness*, 161.

action, visited her New York apartment. Maurin had gotten Day's address from the editor of *Commonweal* magazine. Maurin spoke to Day about his wish to cultivate a society rooted in the teachings of the gospel: "The kind of society," he explained, "where it is easier for people to be good."[4]

Maurin suggested that they start a newspaper to promote social revolution based on the teachings of Christ. Day embraced the idea. Maurin originally wanted to call the paper the *Catholic Radical*, but with her Communist background, Dorothy insisted on calling it the *Catholic Worker*. The Paulist Press printed 2,500 copies of the eight-page paper for $57, and on May 1, 1932, the *Catholic Worker* was distributed on Union Square. The paper still sells for one penny per copy—the same price that it sold for when first printed. In its pages, Day wrote about poverty, the plight of the working class, labor strikes, and nonviolent social change. She also wrote about revolutionary movements of the poor around the world, including the revolution led by Nicaragua's General Augusto César Sandino.

> The work that we were engaged in was to publicize and raise funds for General Sandino, who was resisting American aggression in Nicaragua. Our marines were hunting him in the mountains, and the work of our committee was to raise funds and medical supplies. I did the publicity.[5]

The *Catholic Worker* continues to report on contemporary liberation movements of poor and indigenous people around the world, including the Zapatistas of Mexico and the Landless Workers' Movement in Brazil.

In the 1950s Day publicly protested New York's civil-defense drills because she viewed participation in the drills as blind acceptance of the inevitability of war and as a way of sustaining the illusion that nuclear war was survivable. Her commitment to making peace was rooted in noncooperation with systems of violence and with support for those suffering the injustices of poverty and war. At the age of 76, Day was arrested for the last time while supporting César Chavez and migrant farm workers in California. Chavez himself said,

4. Ibid., 170. Maurin quotes from the preamble of the Industrial Workers of the World constitution.

5. Ellsberg, *Dorothy Day*, 190.

It makes us very proud that Dorothy's last trip to jail took place in Fresno, California, with the farm workers. The summer of 1973 was probably the most painful period we have gone through—the union's future existence was being decided in the strike and later in the boycott. Thousands of farm workers went to jail that summer rather than obey unconstitutional injunctions against picketing, hundreds were injured, dozens were shot and two were killed. And Dorothy came to be with us in Fresno, along with nearly a hundred priests and nuns and lay people.[6]

Dorothy Day authored a number of books, including *The Eleventh Virgin* (1924), *On Pilgrimage* (1948), *From Union Square to Rome* (1938), and her 1959 autobiography, *The Long Loneliness.* She based her writing, as well as her participation in civil disobedience and nonviolent direct actions, on a desire to end war and poverty and to cultivate communities based in love and compassion.

Embracing Christianity

Although during her childhood Dorothy Day experienced very little religious life, she felt drawn to understanding and developing spirituality. In her autobiography, Day compares her own spiritual sense to that of Kiriloff, a character in Dostoevsky's *The Possessed*: "All my life I have been haunted by God."[7] As a child she attended services at an Episcopalian church but was fascinated by the discipline of Catholicism. She experienced her first "impulse toward Catholicism" when she observed her friend Kathryn's mother in deep prayer.

In the front bedroom Mrs. Barrett was on her knees, saying her prayers. She turned to tell me that Kathryn and the children had all gone to the store and went on with her praying. And I felt a warm burst of love toward Mrs. Barrett that I have never forgotten, a feeling of gratitude and happiness that still warms my heart when I remem-

6. Ellsberg, *Dorothy Day*, 253.
7. Day, *Long Loneliness*, 11.

ber her. She had God, and there was beauty and joy in her life.[8]

Beauty in the world pointed Day towards the spiritual realm. The fact that we can sense physical beauty reminded her of the Creator of all beauty and life. She enjoyed the natural beauty abounding around her small home on the beach on Staten Island and devoted her life to making the world more beautiful. The joy of giving birth to her daughter changed Dorothy Day's life. Tamar Theresa was born on March 3, 1927, and on December 28, 1927, Day officially converted to Catholicism.

> Those ten days that I was in the hospital [after Tamar's birth] . . . I was supremely happy. If I had written the greatest book, composed the greatest symphony, painted the most beautiful painting, or carved the most exquisite figure, I could not have felt more the exalted creator than I did when they placed my child in my arms. To think that this thing of beauty, sighing gently in my arms, reaching her little mouth for my breast, clutching at me with her tiny beautiful hands, had come from my flesh, was my own child![9]

However, Dorothy Day's entrance into to the Roman Catholic Church involved great internal and interpersonal conflict. Her common-law husband, Forster Batterham, a devoted anarchist, did not share her interest in spirituality, and opposed any affiliation with organized religions. In addition, he opposed bringing children into a world rife with violence and poverty. Day knew that her joining the Church would end their relationship.

> I never regretted for one minute the step which I had taken in becoming a Catholic, but I repeat that for a year there was little joy for me as the struggle continued.[10]

Day recognized that the Catholic Church was not engaged enough in stopping wars and addressing suffering from poverty and hunger. She saw that religious and political extremism often caused

8. Ellsberg, *Dorothy Day*, 11–12.

9. Ibid., 187–88.

10. Ibid., 40.

violence, but she had faith in the fundamental base of all religious traditions; love.

> Great crimes, it is true, have been committed in the name of human brotherhood; that may serve to obscure the truth, but we must keep on saying it. We must keep on saying it because Love is the reason for our existence.[11]

Dorothy Day prayed and worked not only to help those in need, but also to change what she called "the dirty rotten system."[12] She worked on food lines and advocated a more just economic and social structure where fewer people would lack food, shelter and the opportunity to contribute to life. She wanted a system that would serve the masses, not a system that maintained benefits for a ruling and privileged class, built upon the sweat of an underprivileged majority.

The Power of Compassion and Love

> God is Love. Love casts out fear. Even the most ardent revolutionist, seeking to change the world, to overturn the tables of the money changers, is trying to make a world where it is easier for people to love, to stand in that relationship to each other.[13]

In modern times love has been associated with so many different things that its meaning has become obscured. Dorothy Day and other Christian peacemakers experienced the enormous power of love that transforms individuals, organizations, and societies. She recognized that love and compassion provide antidotes to anger and violence; violence only begets violence, but love creates peace. The all-too-familiar face of romantic love obscures the strong, spiritual aspects of love, rendering them passive and noninfluential. However, Dorothy Day said, "The final word is love."

11. Ellsberg, *Dorothy Day*, 114.

12. Dozens of books and articles give Dorothy credit for this phrase and at catholicworker.com/bookstore/ a black and white poster is available with the phrase, "Our problems stem from our acceptance of this filthy, rotten system." The phrase is described as "Perhaps Dorothy Day's most famous quote." However, I can find no citations of the exact time and place when she wrote or said this.

13. Ellsberg, *Dorothy Day*, 213.

> Teilhard de Chardin writes: "Someday, after mastering the winds, the waves, the tides and gravity, we shall harness for God the energies of love and then for the second time in the history of the world, man will discover fire."[14]

She wanted Catholics and other Christians in the United States to put compassion and love at the heart of their lives. Her own life and actions remind us that when one person is suffering, we are all suffering. By embracing poverty and simplicity, she wanted to eliminate her own privilege.

> Love of brother means voluntary poverty, stripping one's self, putting off the old man, denying one's self. It also means non-participation in those comforts and luxuries, which have been manufactured by the exploitation of others. While our brothers suffer, we must suffer with them. While our brothers suffer from lack of necessities, we will refuse to enjoy comforts.[15]

Day's teachings about compassion—understanding or taking on the suffering of others—can seem repugnant, particularly in a Western culture that seeks pleasure and avoids pain. We might ask, "Who would want to follow a path that involves suffering when they could avoid it?" But when we look more deeply, it is clear that simply being alive involves suffering. Even if we try to avoid suffering, it finds us. In fact, those trying the hardest to avoid it often suffer the most. The more we maximize individual pleasure and minimize individual suffering, the more we tend to suffer.

Within this context or reality we can best understand Christ's teachings about human suffering, and Dorothy Day's applications of them. The nonviolent way to peace, life, and salvation as taught by Jesus illuminates *how* to suffer, and how to use problems and suffering to grow spiritually and psychologically. If we learn to suffer as Jesus Christ taught, we will gain freedom from violence.

Like Jesus, Dorothy Day saw that suffering and compassion are inseparable. Compassion for those who suffer means suffering *with* them. Jesus' crucifixion for the forgiveness of all our sins epitomizes such suffering. Compassion allows us to understand the feelings of

14. Ellsberg, *Dorothy Day*, 353.

15. Ibid., 229.

others and to eliminate the illusion that we are separate and disconnected from one another.

Like all the great nonviolent Christian peacemakers, Dorothy Day had a great capacity for positive self-transformation. She recognized that the transformation of society requires the transformation of individuals, and that the people we each have the greatest potential to transform are ourselves. Day cultivated in herself the desire to go beyond the mundane desires of her own ego and to develop empathy and compassion for others. In turn, she understood the interconnection between all beings and the joy that comes with cherishing others more than oneself. Repentance, prayer, discussions, retreats, and worship in church led to constructive and positive thoughts, feelings, attitudes, and actions. Day was eager to identify actions of her own that could be improved and aspects of herself that could be transformed, all of which she held with a sense of self-love and selfless service.

> I suppose it is a grace not to be able to have time to take or derive satisfaction in the work we are doing. In what time I have, my impulse is to self-criticism and examination of conscience and I am constantly humiliated at my own imperfections and at my halting progress. Perhaps I deceive myself here, too and excuse my lack of recollection. But I do know how small I am and how little I can do and I beg You, Lord, to help me, for I cannot help myself.[16]

The most important tool the nonviolent Christian peacemaker can use is love. No matter what our spiritual tradition—Christian, Jew, Muslim, Buddhist, Hindu, Sufi, or any other—we can best measure our spiritual growth and maturity by our love for others. As Dorothy was reported to have often said, "Love is the measure by which we shall be judged."[17]

16. Ellsberg, *Dorothy Day*, 64.
17. Ibid., 265.

The Catholic Worker Movement:
Integration of Social Change and Spiritual Growth

> "The most significant thing about *The Catholic Worker* is poverty," some say. The most significant thing is community, others say. We are not alone any more. But the final word is love. . . . We cannot love God unless we love each other.[18]

The congruence or integrity between a person's ideals and the way that she lives her life indicates her level of spiritual growth and maturity. Like her beloved St. Francis, Dorothy Day preached that we can truly know only what we experience personally. Her words about engaging in "works of mercy" ring true because she integrated mercy and compassion into her own actions. Dorothy Day and the Catholic Worker Movement challenged the Catholic Church to address war, poverty, and violence more directly while simultaneously challenging radical activists and organizations to incorporate spiritual components of love and compassion.

> The old I. W. W. slogan "An injury to one is an injury to all" is another way of saying what St. Paul said almost two thousand years ago. "We are all members of one another, and when the health of one member suffers, the health of the whole body is lowered." And the converse is true. We can indeed hold each other up in prayer. Excuse this preaching. I am preaching to myself too.[19]

Meeting Peter Maurin in December 1931 changed the direction of Dorothy Day's life. Maurin had grown up in a French Catholic peasant family, one of twenty-two children. He was educated in Catholic schools and for a while joined the Christian Brothers.

> My life has been divided into two parts. The first twenty-five years were foundering, years of joy and sorrow, it is true, but certainly with a sense of that insecurity one hears so much about these days. I did not know in what I believed, though I tried to serve a cause. Five years after I

---

18. Day, *Long Loneliness*, 285.
19. Ellsberg, *Dorothy Day*, 345.

became a Catholic I met Peter Maurin and his story must play a great part in this work because he was my master and I was his disciple; he gave me "a way of life and instruction," and to explain what has come to be known as "The Catholic Worker Movement" in the Church throughout the world, I must write of him.[20]

Day sensed Maurin's unconditional love for others, and she appreciated his outspoken criticism of the institutions and activities that had corrupted people's lives and interfered with their happiness: the state, capitalism, war, usury, and the loss of a philosophy of work. Maurin embraced poverty, sustaining himself by living on the land. The Catholic Worker Movement established urban "houses of hospitality" and some farms to the same end. The first houses of hospitality were Maryhouse and St. Joseph's House. Today there are about 185 Catholic Worker houses worldwide.[21]

> Peter made you feel a sense of his mission as soon as you met him. He did not begin by tearing down, or by painting so intense a picture of misery and injustice that you burned to change the world. Instead, he aroused in you a sense of your own capacities for work, for accomplishment. He made you feel that you and all men had great and generous hearts with which to love God. If you once recognized this fact in yourself you would expect and find it in others. "The art of human contacts," Peter called it happily. But it was seeing Christ in others without being able to see Him. Blessed is he that believes without seeing.[22]

Peter Maurin became well known for the poetic style of the "easy essays" that he contributed regularly to the *Catholic Worker* newspaper. The first edition featured the following short verse:

> The world would become better off
> if people tried to become better.
> And people would become better
> if they stopped trying to become better off.[23]

20. Day, *Long Loneliness*, 11.
21. "Catholic Worker Movement"
22. Ellsberg, *Dorothy Day*, 44.
23. Ibid., xxv.

The paper often printed the goal of the Catholic Worker Movement: "to realize in the individual and society the expressed and implied teachings of Christ."[24] Day understood that Christ taught that love must be concrete and active. She appreciated Catholic "private morality" but criticized the church's lack of a "social or political morality." She noticed that acceptance of Christ and surrender to his will had been manipulated to convince the poor and victims of war that "God meant it to be so."[25] On the contrary, Dorothy Day and Peter Maurin were striving to create heaven on earth in the present and were not satisfied with an interpretation of the Gospels that held that heaven would come to the meek only later, in the afterlife. Overall, the *Catholic Worker* newspaper voiced an increasingly pacifist, antiwar position that many Catholics found unfamiliar.

> The fundamental means of the Catholic Worker are voluntary poverty and manual labor, a spirit of detachment from all things, a sense of the primacy of the spiritual, which makes the rest easy. "His praise should be ever in our mouth."[26]

Nonviolence Is Christian

> We oppose all use of violence as un-Christian. We do not believe in persuading scabs with clubs. They are workers, too, and the reason they are scabs is because the work of organization has been neglected.[27]

As Day understood it, Jesus' teachings prohibited participation in and support for war in any form, whether in planning, rehearsing, or paying for it. She believed that Jesus had taught nonviolent peacemaking as a practical and principled alternative to all forms and levels of violence. She integrated the two primary aspects of nonviolent Christian peacemaking: opposing violence and engaging in constructive peacemaking.

24. Ellsberg, *Dorothy Day*, xvi.
25. Ibid., 237.
26. Ibid.,113–14.
27. Ibid., 243.

Dorothy Day encouraged young people to become conscientious objectors and to refuse to take up arms. The FBI questioned her about her involvement in such antiwar activities. She spoke out against U.S. participation in both world wars, against capital punishment, and against the mass imprisonment of people of color and of the poor.

Her nonviolent opposition to U.S. involvement in World War II after the Japanese attacks on Pearl Harbor was not popular. The vast majority of Americans believed that only violent retribution would end the war, and that firebombing German cities and dropping nuclear bombs on Japan would bring peace. Nevertheless, Dorothy Day opposed the violence of the U.S. military *and* the atrocities of Nazi Germany and imperialist Japan: As one *Catholic Worker* headline read,

> We are Un-American; We Are Catholics.[28]

Although she celebrated the end of World War II, Dorothy Day was concerned that the violent tactics used to stop violence would create an atmosphere of fear and hatred that would permeate international relations. She feared that retributive or preventative violence would encourage the acceptance of violence and war as strategies for world peace and would also determine the way the next war might be waged. So she sensed the beginning of what came to be known as the cold war.

> Until we ourselves as followers of Christ abjure the use of war as a means of achieving justice and truth, we Catholics are going to get nowhere in criticizing men who are using war to change the social order.[29]

Day openly challenged and explicitly opposed the illusion of the survivability of a nuclear war, and in June 1955 she refused to take part in the first U.S. air-raid drills. She considered them a public morality play that ingrained fear of enemies and cultivated an illusory hope of surviving nuclear war by closing windows, hiding under desks, or running into the subway. She and others in the Catholic Worker community actively opposed all rehearsals for nuclear vio-

28. Ellsberg, *Dorothy Day*, 270.
29. Ibid., 304.

lence, even when their fellow citizens threatened them, or when the police arrested them.

> In the name of Jesus, who is God, who is Love, we will
> not obey this order to pretend, to evacuate, to hide . . .
> We will not be drilled into fear . . . . We do not have faith
> in God if we depend upon the Atom Bomb. [30]

Simultaneously Day considered the development of weapons a waste of funds that could be better spent alleviating the suffering of the hungry and homeless. She and many others in the Catholic Worker community refused to pay war taxes, largely by not earning any taxable income. Day advocated and practiced war-tax resistance as part of her Christian responsibility not to support or otherwise participate in killing. On a practical level, she also knew—as do many who lack her courage to follow through on their convictions—that wars run on tax money. If nobody paid for them, wars would stop. As a disciple of Jesus, Day was careful not to pay for the military violence that she opposed. Such war-tax resistance is a traditional aspect of the tenet, "do no harm." Ammon Hennacy, a fellow Catholic Worker and colleague of Day's summed it up by saying, "If we pay taxes, we pay for the bomb."[31]

Dorothy Day did not celebrate the atomic bombings of Hiroshima and Nagasaki, as did President Harry Truman and some of the scientists and academic and industrial leaders who had helped craft the nuclear weapons: "We have created destruction," she wrote of the bombings that leveled two Japanese cities and left over two hundred thousand dead.[32]

While most U.S. citizens celebrated the end of the war—and the beginning of a new global military hegemony—Dorothy Day was among the first to understand and articulate the parallels of the atomic bombings with the Nazi Holocaust. She compared the fiery

---

30. Forest, *Love Is the Measure*, 98.

31. Ellsberg, *Dorothy Day*, 138.

32. Ibid., 267. Frank Barnaby, "Effects of the Atomic Bombings," writes: "The total number of people killed by Little Boy and Fat Man probably exceeds 250,000 . . ." The BBC reports, "The bombs which hit Nagasaki and Hiroshima, in a US bid to force Japan to surrender in 1945, killed about 240,000 people." BBC Online, July 1, 2007 http://news.bbc.co.uk/2/hi/asia-pacific/6258190.stm.

death of the Japanese to the killing of Jews and others in Nazi ovens. She pointed to the contradiction between Jesus' teachings of love and compassion, of nonresistance to evil and of treating your enemy as yourself, with the use of atomic violence. She warned against accepting war as a way of life.

Dorothy Day opposed the U.S. military actions in Vietnam. She also influenced and supported other nonviolent Christian peacemakers who opposed that war, such as Liz MacAlister, Thomas Merton, and the brothers Daniel and Philip Berrigan (members of the "Catonsville Nine," a group of Catholic activists arrested in 1969 for pouring blood on draft cards and burning them in Catsonville, Maryland). Dorothy engaged in and supported a variety of resistance actions ranging from attending demonstrations and writing political statements to counseling potential conscientious objectors. Her actions displeased many *Catholic Worker* readers and supporters. But her commitment to truth, nonviolent peacemaking, and the rest of Jesus' way was more important to her than holding a popular position. She believed in democracy, but she believed more in peace and in contributing to life.

Nonviolent Christian Revolution

> I am sure that God did not intend that there be so many poor. The class structure is of *our* making and by *our* consent, not His, and we must do what we can to change it. So we are urging revolutionary change.[33]

Dorothy Day perceived revolution as a personal *and* political affair that did not come as a single upheaval but was practiced daily through prayer, faith, and action. She referred to the continuous and long-term nature of social change and spiritual growth as a "permanent revolution."[34] She appreciated the Communist critique of capitalism but disagreed with their means of violent class warfare to achieve peaceful ends. She also disagreed with the antireligious sentiments of Communism and, indeed, discovered that revolutionary social change was linked to personal liberation and spiritual growth.

33. Ellsberg, *Dorothy Day*, 111.
34. Day, *Long Loneliness*, 186.

> This work of ours toward a new heaven and a new earth
> shows a correlation between the material and the spiritu-
> al, and, of course, recognizes the primacy of the spiritual.
> Food for the body is not enough. There must be food for
> the soul.[35]

For Dorothy Day, Peter Maurin, and the contemporary
Catholic Worker Movement, works of mercy include not only meeting the immediate needs of people (such as food and shelter) but also
working to create a society based on peace and justice. All aspects
of Dorothy Day's work to provide food, shelter, and clothing to the
poor, and to dismantle the systems of war and oppression, flowed
from her love for Jesus and her Christian faith.

> The Catholic, the Christian, must outdo in zeal, in self-sac-
> rifice, in dedication, in service for the common good those
> who are following the teachings of Marxism-Leninism.[36]

Dorothy Day viewed her work and that of the Catholic Worker
Movement as a peaceful, Christian alternative to Communism. She
was grateful for the learning she had received by studying Communism
and from her experiences with colleagues who embraced the class
analysis of Karl Marx, but she found a deeper connection and possibility for social change in the teachings of Christ.

> First of all, let it be remembered that I speak as an
> ex-Communist and one who has not testified before
> congressional committees, nor written works on the
> Communist conspiracy. I can say with warmth that I
> loved the people I worked with and learned much from
> them. They helped me to find God in His poor, in His
> abandoned ones, as I had not found Him in Christian
> churches.[37]

Dorothy understood the relationship between poverty and the
division of labor in the United States and agreed that ownership of
the means of production was confined to a small, elite upper class.
An economic and class analysis instilled in her a desire to end the sys-

35. Ellsberg, *Dorothy Day*, 91.
36. Ibid., 311.
37. Ibid., 271.

tem that perpetuated a minority living in comfort and wealth while a majority struggled to meet basic needs.

We want to make "the rich poor and the poor holy."[38]

Day felt that rather than violence, the love and compassion Jesus exemplified was a more beneficial and successful motivating force for the revolutionary personal transformation and social change required for the blossoming of peace and justice. She felt strongly that violent tactics would only bring more violence, and she instead chose nonviolent direct action as her means *and* ends for peace and justice.

> Certainly we disagree over and over again with the means chosen to reach their ends, because, as we have repeated many a time, the means become the end.[39]

Dorothy Day faced the spiritual and psychological challenge of seeing Jesus in everyone she encountered: from those who were living in material and spiritual poverty to those who were planning wars and developing weapons of mass destruction. Her compassion extended to all, and her commitment to a nonviolent Christian revolution inspired many who have followed in her footsteps. Of course, many socialist and Communist organizers criticized Dorothy's religious commitment to revolution and her nonviolent tactics.

> They [Communists] are protesting against man's brutality to man, and at the same time they perpetuate it. It is like having one more war to end all wars. We disagree with this technique of class war, without which the Communist says the brotherhood of man can never be achieved. "Nothing will be achieved until the worker rises up in arms and forcibly takes the position that is his," the Communist says. "Your movement, which trusts to peaceful means, radical though it may seem, is doomed to failure."[40]

Sooner or later, most activists come to know that the state can respond to nonviolent change in dramatic and violent ways. Like those of other compassion-based activists, Dorothy Day's ideas and

38. Ellsberg, *Dorothy Day*, 272.
39. Ibid., 271–72.
40. Ibid., 243.

actions turned radical when she experienced state-sponsored violence. In 1937 she witnessed police attacking a rally of steelworkers during their strike at the Republic Steel Company on the south side of Chicago, killing ten and wounding 160.

> Try to imagine this mass of people—men, women, and children—picketing, as they have a right to do, coming up to the police line and being suddenly shot into, not by one hysterical policeman, but by many. Ten were killed and one hundred were taken to the hospital wounded. Tear gas and clubs supplied by the Republic Steel Company were used. I am trying to picture this scene to our readers because I have witnessed these things firsthand, and I know the horror of them. I was on a picket line when the "radical" squad shot into the line and pursued the fleeing picketers down the streets, knocking them down and kicking and beating them. I, too, have fled down the streets to escape the brutality and vicious hatred of the "law" for those whom they consider "radical." And by the police anyone who protests injustice, who participates in labor struggles, is considered a radical.[41]

Dorothy Day protested this and other incidents of police brutality. She reported them in the *Catholic Worker*, gave public talks, and protested directly to the police commissioner because, as she put it, "the only way to stop such brutality is to arouse a storm of protest against it."[42] Day was one of the most influential U.S. Roman Catholics and Christians of the twentieth century. The twenty-first-century Christian church has much to learn from this woman of peace, prayer. and service. In her writing and in her life, Dorothy Day showed that human beings can find peace and offer it to the world by following Jesus' way as it is revealed in the gospel and as it is represented within the Christian tradition of nonviolent action and our own consciences.

41. Ellsberg, *Dorothy Day*, 245.
42. Ibid.

6

Thomas Merton

THOMAS MERTON, a monk, a contemplative, an author, and a revolutionary realist focused his heart and mind on the critical issues of war, peace, and human survival. He had the ability to communicate not only with Christians but also with people of all religious traditions and with those of no religion at all. Merton's life and work offer an example of the possibility of integrating spiritual growth and social change by combining contemplation, writing, and nonviolent direct action. He worked to clarify Christian nonviolent peacemaking methods, principles, and processes, and pointed to the common ground that peacemaking shares in universal spiritual traditions. Merton wrote over sixty books including *No Man Is an Island* (1978), *Faith and Violence: Christian Teaching and Christian Practice* (1968), *Mystics and Zen Masters* (1967), and his 1948 autobiography, *The Seven Storey Mountain.*

Thomas Merton was born on January 30, 1915, in Prades, France. His American mother, Ruth, and New Zealander father, Owen, were both artists dedicated to a simple lifestyle, and they raised Thomas Merton and his younger brother, John Paul, in Europe. Owen, a painter, made financial ends meet by gardening and playing the organ at a local church and movie theater. Ruth was an active Quaker. In 1916 the family moved to the United States, partly due to their opposition to the First World War. Thomas' mother died when he was only six years old, and his father died from cancer just before Merton's sixteenth birthday.

Merton attended Cambridge University for one year and than returned to the United States to live with his grandparents. He later completed bachelor's and master's degrees at Columbia University in New York City.

Merton registered as a conscientious objector during the U.S. military draft for World War II. He had been willing to serve in noncombatant roles, for example as a medic, but his application was rejected. In his early twenties, Merton converted to Catholicism and felt the desire to become a monk but was rejected by the Franciscans when he revealed that he had been expelled from Cambridge University after fathering a child out of wedlock. At the age of twenty-six, Merton was accepted as a choir novice into the Order of Cistercians of The Strict Observance (Trappists) at the Abbey of Gesthemani in Kentucky. He was given the name Fr. Louis. Ten years later, he became a U.S. citizen.

During the 1960s and '70s, as the Vietnam War intensified, Merton strengthened his commitment to nonviolent Christian peace-making. He expanded his focus on contemplation and prayer and directed his writing and public actions more clearly towards peace. At the monastery he was encouraged to write. He befriended many Christians of that time who were practicing nonviolence, including Daniel and Philip Berrigan, Dorothy Day, Jim Forest, and the community of Catholic Workers. Merton actively participated with the Fellowship of Reconciliation and the Catholic Peace Fellowship, which later became Pax Christi. Merton's aversion to bloodshed became even more personal when his brother, John Paul, a member of the Royal Canadian Air Force, was killed in Vietnam. Although Merton appreciated the ideals upon which U.S. democracy was founded, he criticized the violent political and economic strategies of the United States government.

Merton's Trappist superiors disagreed with his political analysis, and in 1962 they attempted to censor his writings about war and peace. He continued producing and circulating "unpublished" writings, and many believe that his work during this period influenced *Pacem in Terris*, Pope John XXIII's encyclical on Christianity, peace-making, and world peace. The ban on Merton's peace writings was lifted in 1964 when the Trappist leadership changed.

> So instead of loving what you think is peace, love other men and love God above all. And instead of hating the people you think are warmakers, hate the appetites and the disorder in your own soul, which are the causes of war.

If you love peace, then hate injustice, hate tyranny, hate greed—but hate these things *in yourself,* not in another.[1]

Merton, who encouraged interfaith dialogue and cooperation, was deeply influenced by Eastern wisdom traditions. In 1968 he traveled to India, where he met His Holiness The Dalai Lama. Merton wrote in *The Asian Journal* of the profound effect the Buddha statues in Polonnaruwa, Sri Lanka, had upon him. He then traveled to Bangkok, Thailand, where he had been invited to speak at a conference on modern monasticism. On December 10, 1968, he died when he stepped out of his bath and touched an electric fan with faulty wiring.

Theology of Love: Truth and Compassion

Thomas Merton recognized the incredibly destructive power in the human propensity for violence, as well as the constructive power of love in serving others compassionately. Merton said that the contemplative has the special task of being as aware as possible of the real and the true, and that this clarity and pure awareness is the monk's primary service to the world. He followed the path of Christian mysticism, a tradition based in direct experience with God and on personal knowledge of the interconnection of all life. He also understood that theologies of love had been corrupted and used to legitimize the violence of the rich and powerful.

> A theology of love cannot afford to be sentimental. It cannot afford to preach edifying generalities about charity, while identifying "peace" with mere established power and legalized violence against the oppressed. A theology of love cannot be allowed merely to serve the interests of the rich and powerful, justifying their wars, their violence and their bombs, while exhorting the poor and underprivileged to practice patience, meekness, longsuffering and to solve their problems, if at all, non-violently.[2]

Merton saw that all violence begins in the mind, and that it is the violence within ourselves that we can reduce with the great-

1. Merton, *New Seeds of Contemplation*, 122.
2. Merton, *Faith and Violence*, 8–9.

est success. Merton viewed our habitual tendencies of anger, greed and war as addictions that could be overcome. He himself strove to become ever more nonviolent in thought and action.

> The human race today is like an alcoholic who knows that drink will destroy him and yet always has "good reasons" why he must continue drinking. Such is man in his fatal addiction to war. He is not really capable of seeing a constructive alternative to war. If this task of building a peaceful world is the most important task of our time, it is also the most difficult. It will, in fact, require far more discipline, more sacrifice, more planning, more thought, more cooperation and more heroism than war ever demanded. The task of ending war is in fact the greatest challenge to human courage and intelligence. Can we meet this challenge?[3]

Merton observed that violence in our families and between nations stems from, and reflects, the violence within our individual hearts and minds. If we want to promote peace and well-being, we must come to know real peace within ourselves. We must grow into more spiritually and psychologically developed and mature human beings. Thomas Merton, the monk and priest, believed that the more we know the peace of Christ, the better we can work nonviolently for peace in the world.

> The monk searches not only his own heart: he plunges deep into the heart of the world of which he remains a part although he seems to have "left" it. In reality the monk abandons the world only to listen more intently to the deepest and most neglected voices that proceed from its inner depth . . . . This is precisely the monk's chief service to the world: this silence, this questioning, this humble and courageous exposure to what the world ignores about itself—both good and evil.[4]

Merton advocated that we meet the challenge of violence with compassion—the only alternative to the strategies of punishment and revenge. He recognized different levels of violence, noting the

3. Merton, *Nonviolent Alternative*, 16.
4. Merton, *Contemplative Prayer*, 23, 25.

subtle and habitual human desire to eliminate one's "enemy." He wondered if we would be able to change our ways of thinking in time to avoid disaster.

> All still assume that the only way to peace is to abolish the enemy—or reduce him to helplessness. And this is in fact what the average citizen still believes. The mere problem of getting people to think otherwise is in fact an awesome challenge to human courage and intelligence. Can we meet this challenge? Do we have the moral strength and the faith that are required to make so drastic a change in a short time?[5]

We can reduce the internal causes of violence and the external manifestations of poverty and war not through physical force but through spiritual forces of nonviolence and compassion. Merton often wrote of the strength of surrendering to God, or truth.

> The true solutions are not those which we force upon life in accordance with our theories, but those which life itself provides for those who dispose themselves to receive the truth.[6]

Merton based his writings and actions in Jesus' teachings on love and truth. He believed that all Christians have the duty to consider their own relationship to violence—especially regarding their own profession, nation, religion, and society. Like Martin Luther King Jr., Mohandas Gandhi, and Dorothy Day, Merton saw that contemporary violence arises, for the most part, from economic disparity manifested as the poverty and debt that social systems and political institutions cause. He also pointed out that some of the "most respected" religious institutions accept or even perpetrate much of this violence. He challenged everyone, especially Christians, to become aware of the hypocrisy of investing in, working for, and profiting from violence.

5. Merton, *Faith and Violence*, 42.
6. Merton, *Raids on the Unspeakable*, 60–61.

> Never was opposition to war more urgent and more
> necessary than now. Never was religious protest so
> badly needed.[7]

Through contemplation and self-inquiry, Merton became aware
of the depths at which violence lurks in the human heart and mind.
He avoided demonizing those with whom he disagreed and instead
strove to cultivate compassion for everyone. He recognized that we
all suffer from self-deception and habitual tendencies to act selfishly
and violently.

> We never see the one truth that would help us begin to
> solve our ethical and political problems: that we are *all*
> more or less wrong, that we are *all* at fault, *all* limited and
> obstructed by our mixed motives, our self-deception, our
> greed, our self-righteousness and our tendency to aggres-
> sivity and hypocrisy.[8]

For Merton, the struggle for personal and collective freedom
and peace begins by recognizing and cultivating the power of love.
Love can sustain life and provide an antidote to selfishness, hatred,
and delusion.

> We must all believe in life and in peace. We must believe
> in the power of love. We must recognize that our being
> itself is grounded in love: that is to say that we come into
> being because we are loved and because we are meant to
> love others. The failure to believe this and to live accord-
> ingly creates instead a deep mistrust, a suspicion of oth-
> ers, a hatred of others, and a failure to love. When a man
> attempts to live by and for himself alone, he becomes a
> little "island" of hate, greed, suspicion, fear, desire. Then
> his whole outlook on life is falsified. All his judgments
> are affected by this untruth. In order to recover the true
> perspective, which is that of love and compassion, he
> must once again learn, in simplicity, trust and peace, that
> "no man is an island."[9]

---

7. Merton, *Nonviolent Alternative*, 107.

8. Merton, *New Seeds of Contemplation*, 115–16.

9. Merton, *Nonviolent Alternative*, 65–66.

Merton realized that corrupted theologies of love and compassion served the selfish desires of individuals and governments who had come to equate love and compassion with acquiescence to the status quo.

> The temptation of our day is to equate "love" and "conformity"—passive subservience to the mass-mind or to the organization.[10]

According to Merton, Christian love is not a pleasurable feeling but is action based on our willingness to understand others and to consider their needs and interests to be as important as our own. Such love and compassion, or *agape*, creates peace within those who cultivate such relationships with others.

Spirituality and Social Change

In the United States Thomas Merton challenged Christians to transform their social and political climate in much the same way that Gandhi had challenged the Hindus of India. Both Gandhi and Merton urged their brothers and sisters to recognize that their religion had become complacent and was no longer true to its own teachings.

> What is required is a spiritual upheaval such as we seldom see recorded in history. But such things have happened, and let us hope we have not gone so far that they will not happen again.[11]

Both Merton and Gandhi worked for peace and justice because of their commitment to God and their appreciation of the sacredness of all life. Merton saw that Christian thinking had to transform political attitudes and address the social problems of the day. For him, spiritual growth and social change went hand in hand and supported each other.

> This means overcoming the "split" between the sacred and the profane, the spiritual and the political.[12]

10. Merton, *New Seeds of Contemplation*, 53.
11. Merton, *Faith and Violence*, 118.
12. Merton, *Nonviolent Alternative*, 93.

Merton agreed with Karl Marx that religion *can* become an opiate of the people, and Merton warned that religions can easily become corrupted, numbing believers' senses to the suffering of violence and oppression.

> Christ Our Lord did not come to bring peace to the world as a kind of spiritual tranquilizer. He brought to His disciples a vocation and as a task, to struggle in the world of violence to establish His peace not only in their own hearts but in society itself.[13]

Merton did not fear the truth of critics and opponents of Christianity, who pointed out that such "narcotic religion" ignores the poor and serves the interests of privilege, wealth, and the status quo. Such narcotic religion perpetuates violence even while denying it is doing so.

> Without true, deep contemplative aspirations, without a total love for God and an uncompromising thirst for his truth, religion tends in the end to become an opiate.[14]

For Merton, contemplative prayer provided the antidote to opiate religion. Contemplating the love of God, longing for the coming of Christ, and thirsting for the manifestation of God's glory led him to inner truth. These characteristically "contemplative" and eschatological aspirations of the Christian heart are the very essence of monastic prayer.

> But the activity of a contemplative must be born of his contemplation and must resemble it. Everything he does outside of contemplation ought to reflect the luminous tranquility of his interior life.[15]

Thomas Merton found that truth and love are not only the goals in nonviolent peacemaking but are also the means. Merton knew that since each of us can only see part of truth, the process of nonviolent peacemaking involves acknowledging and understanding each others' perspectives, knowing that each holds a piece of a larger truth.

13. Merton, *Nonviolent Alternative*, 13.

14. Merton, *Contemplative Prayer*, 116.

15. Merton, *New Seeds of Contemplation*, 192.

The mystic and the spiritual man who in our day remain indifferent to the problems of their fellow men, who are not fully capable of facing those problems, will find themselves inevitably involved in the same ruin. They will suffer the same deceptions, be implicated in the same crimes. They will go down to ruin with the same blindness and the same insensitivity to the presence of evil. They will be deaf to the voice crying in the wilderness, for they will have listened to some other, more comforting voice, of their own making. This is the penalty of evasion and complacency.[16]

Recognizing this universality of spiritual traditions did not distract Merton from his commitment to the teachings and methods of Christianity. Indeed, many activists for social change find that an awareness of the universality of nonviolent, compassion-based peacemaking enhances their understanding and application of the teachings from their particular tradition.

Merton saw this universal spiritual tradition exemplified in the life teachings of Gandhi, a Hindu from India, and also in two remarkable Buddhist peacemakers: His Holiness The Dalai Lama, the spiritual and political leader of Tibet exiled after the Chinese invasion and takeover; and Thich Nhat Hanh, the Zen Buddhist monk from Vietnam, whom Martin Luther King Jr. nominated for the Nobel Peace Prize in 1967. During the height of the war in Vietnam, Merton called Thich Nhat Hanh "my brother":

I have said Nhat Hanh is my brother, and it is true. We are both monks, and we have lived the monastic life for about the same number of years. We are both poets, both existentialists. I have far more in common with Nhat Hanh than I have with many Americans.[17]

Even as Merton's appreciation of Hinduism and Buddhism deepened through his studying these religious traditions and meeting some of their practitioners, Merton's Christian faith and prayer deepened. Liberating oneself leads one to help liberate others, and

16. Merton, *Faith and Violence*, 67–68.
17. Merton, *Faith and Violence*, 108.

vice versa, infinitely. Spiritual growth has a social context; personal liberation and political freedom feed each other.

> The spiritual or interior life is not an exclusively private affair. . . . The spiritual life of one person is simply the life of all manifesting itself in him. While it is very necessary to emphasize the truth that as the person deepens his own thought in silence he enters into a deeper understanding of and communion with the spirit of his entire people (or of his Church), it is also important to remember that as he becomes engaged in the crucial struggles of his people, in seeking justice and truth together with his brother, he tends to liberate the truth in himself by seeking true liberty for all.[18]

Nonviolent Christian Revolution

> The Christian . . . as a follower of Christ, must be a peacemaker.[19]

Merton loved the Roman Catholic Church and the Christian faith. Because of this, he was disappointed by Christians who deviated from Jesus' essential teachings. He was particularly critical of the Church during the war in Vietnam, when he saw his country not only deviate from Jesus' peacemaking but actually oppose it. He noted that the U.S. military dropped more bombs on southeast Asia than it did during all of World War II, while Christian leadership in the United States did little to stop the war.[20]

> One of the grave problems of religion in our time is posed by the almost total lack of protest on the part of religious people and clergy in the face of enormous social evils.[21]

Merton pointed out that Christians who tolerated the development or use of nuclear weapons committed blasphemy. He considered support for such potentially omnicidal violence antichristian.

18. Merton, "Gandhi," 6.
19. Merton, *Nonviolent Alternative*, 31.
20. Merton, *Faith and Violence*, 3.
21. Ibid., 129.

In actual fact it seems that Christians, as much as any-body else, are contributing very much to the dangerous tensions and the irrational state of mind which is obsessed with the fear of disaster and is fixated on one hope: nuclear defense. It is Christians who are, as loudly as anyone else, clamoring for an unbeatable missile defense system—all of course in the name of "peace." And it is Christians who, as much as anybody else, are refusing even to consider possible alternatives to this line of action. It is Christians who most loudly and passionately support policies of overkill.[22]

The Christian teachings of forgiveness, compassion, and peace-making are incompatible with nationalism that promotes economic war and violence. In the 1960s Merton saw that the West, once commonly considered Christian, had lost its way.

We are no longer living in a Christian world.... It is a great mistake to identify a nationalistic society that was once officially Christian with Christendom or Christianity. It is a serious error to imagine that because the West was once largely Christian, the cause of the Western nations is now to be identified, without further qualification, with the cause of God. The incentive to do this, and to proceed on this assumption to a nuclear crusade to wipe out Bolshevism, may well be one of the apocalyptic temptations of twentieth-century Christendom.[23]

Merton pointed to the revolutionary power of love as an integral part of Christian peacemaking. He cautioned against the temptation to hate our enemies, reminding us that the teachings of Jesus call on us to love our enemies.

Do not think that you can show your love for Christ by hating those who seem to be His enemies on earth. Suppose they really do hate Him: nevertheless He loves them, and you cannot be united with Him unless you love them too. If you hate the enemies of the Church instead of loving them, you too will run the risk of be-

22. Merton, *Faith and Violence*, 89.
23. Ibid.,13–14.

coming an enemy of the Church, and of Christ; for He said: "Love your enemies," and He also said: "He that is not with me is against me."[24]

Christian revolution demands no death save that of our own separate sense of self. A revolution that seeks to annihilate enemies does not generate social change; it continues a cycle of violence that never builds, and only destroys.

> And yet this tradition [of Christian peacemaking] must always be a revolution because by its very nature it denies the values and standards to which human passion is so powerfully attached. . . . This is the most complete revolution that has ever been preached; in fact, it is the only true revolution, because all the others demand the extermination of somebody else, but this one means the death of the man who, for all practical purposes, you have come to think of as your own self.[25]

Merton saw that Christians could apply the power of Gandhi's *satyagraha* (or "soul-force") to personal and international conflict. He beckoned them to lay aside their material weapons, relying instead on "spiritual arms."

> We believe, precisely, that an essential part of the "good news" is that spiritual weapons are stronger than material ones. Indeed, by spiritual arms, the early Church conquered the entire Roman world. Have we lost our faith in this "sword of the Spirit?" Have we perhaps lost all realization of its very existence?[26]

Merton felt that making international peace must begin by addressing personal and national violence. He cautioned us to not advise others about peace and nonviolent peacemaking until we have experienced peace in ourselves and in our own nation. He warned against the false nonviolence that takes the form of passivity and nationalism.

---

24. Merton, *New Seeds of Contemplation*, 176–77.

25. Ibid.,143–44.

26. Merton, *Nonviolent Alternative*, 115.

> We must frankly face the possibility that the nonvio-
> lence of the European or American preaching Christian
> meekness may conceivably be adulterated by bourgeois
> feelings and by an unconscious desire to preserve the
> status quo against violent upheaval. A real understanding
> of Christian nonviolence (backed up by the evidence of
> history in the Apostolic Age) shows not only that it is a
> *power*, but that it remains perhaps the only really effective
> way of transforming man and human society.[27]

Merton pointed out that preparations for nuclear war grew
from the violence that preceded this preparation. In other words, we
may be afraid of having violence inflicted upon us because of the violence that has been inflicted on others in our name or with our support. Indeed, most of the land that has become the United States was
taken violently from the indigenous population. Estimates of how
many people lived in North and South America prior to European
colonization vary widely from eight million to 100 million, with between five million and 40 million in what is now the United States.[28]
Ironically, many of the original European immigrants themselves
had fled religious and political oppression to settle in America. Until
we take responsibility for our own history of violence, it is bound to
cause suffering.

> Unfortunately, we learned little or nothing about our-
> selves from the Indian wars! . . . But we are left with a
> deep sense of guilt and shame. The record is there. The
> Mill Creek Indians, who were once seen as bloodthirsty
> devils, were peaceful, innocent and deeply wronged
> human beings. In their use of violence they were, so it
> seems, generally very fair. It is we who were the wanton
> murderers, and they who were the innocent victims.[29]

Merton suggested that all citizens of the United States hold
some responsibility for violence perpetrated by our government. Are
we innocent when we pay the taxes that support the development of
nuclear weapons and military violence? Or when we allow corpora-

---

27. Merton, *Nonviolent Alternative*, 212.

28. Stannard, *American Holocaust*, 11.

29. Ibid., 249–50.

tions and governments to destroy nations? He urged us to accept responsibility for our history and our present, and not just criticize those in positions of political power.

> Nowadays it is no longer a question of who is right, but who is at least not criminal, if any of us can say that anymore.[30]

Merton warned against the sanitization of war and other violence by the "white-collar murder machine" of the media and U.S. government.[31] He urged that our personal concerns expand to include not only violence that may occur in our own neighborhood or home but also the much more pervasive devastation of "corporately organized murder."[32]

> The real crimes of modern war are committed not at the front (if any) but in war offices and ministries of defense in which no one ever has to see any blood unless his secretary gets a nosebleed. Modern technological mass murder is not directly visible, like individual murder. It is abstract, corporate, businesslike, cool, free of guilt-feelings and therefore a thousand times more deadly and effective than the eruption of violence out of individual hate. It is this polite, massively organized white-collar murder machine that threatens the world with destruction, not the violence of a few desperate teen-agers in a slum. But our antiquated theology myopically focused on *individual* violence alone fails to see this. It shudders at the phantasm of muggings and killings where a mess is made on our own doorstep, but blesses and canonizes the antiseptic violence of corporately organized murder because it is respectable, efficient, clean, and above all profitable.[33]

Merton saw that war is profitable, and that for American Christians to challenge the violence of their government's wars, they must also challenge the intertwined relationship between industry, academia, politics, and the military.

30. Forest, *Living with Wisdom*, 124.
31. Merton, *Nonviolent Alternative*, 188.
32. Ibid.
33. Merton, *Faith and Violence*, 6–7.

Realize what we are up against. The military-industrial-
political-academic complex, with the mass media at its
disposal, is sold on military defense and the arms race
and is obviously interested in ridiculing or discrediting
all nonmilitary forms of defense—in fact all alternatives
to the arms race.[34]

Merton saw the pitfalls of a *false* nonviolence that still hated
those it opposed or regarded as enemies. He reminds us that loving our enemies must mean not only praying for and loving people
in other countries, but also loving our fellow citizens who oppose
nonviolent peacemaking and perpetuate violence, even if they are
Christians. He did not believe that war and violence are inevitable.

It is therefore supremely important for us not to yield
to despair, abandon ourselves to the "inevitable" and
identify ourselves with "them." Our duty is to refuse to
believe that their way is "inevitable."[35]

Nonviolence: Principles and Methods

Nonviolence . . . is based on that respect for the human
person without which there is no deep and genuine
Christianity.[36]

Merton advocated a method for nonviolent peacemaking that echoed
the "constructive program" that Mohandas Gandhi developed and
practiced in India. The program had two aspects: obstructive and
constructive, with an emphasis on the latter. In both obstructing
violence and constructing nonviolent communication and relationships, we face personal and collective responsibilities for following
and applying Jesus' teachings. Merton warned against the human
tendency to want immediate results and to distrust strategies that
take time. He urged all peacemakers, Christian or otherwise, to cultivate patience.

34. Merton, *Faith and Violence*, 93.
35. Merton, *Raids on the Unspeakable*, 56.
36. Merton, *Nonviolent Alternative*, 216.

> Perhaps the most insidious temptation to be avoided is one which is characteristic of the power structure itself: this fetishism of immediate visible results. Modern society understands "possibilities" and "results" in terms of a superficial and quantitative idea of efficacy. One of the missions of Christian nonviolence is to restore a different standard of practical judgment in social conflicts.[37]

Merton saw that when people develop a sense of compassion and patience, a "different standard of practical judgment" arises. From this connection with inner truths, actions to stop violence and build peace arise naturally. He pointed to the nonviolent actions that obstructed the Nazi violence of World War II.

> The Danes who saved the lives of the Jews in their Nazi-occupied nation were able to do what they did because they were able to make decisions that were based on clear convictions about which they all agreed and which were in accord with the inner truth of man's own rational nature, as well as in accordance with the fundamental law of God in the Old Testament as well as in the Gospel: thou shalt love thy neighbor as thyself. The Danes were able to resist the cruel stupidity of Nazi anti-Semitism because this fundamental truth was *important* to them. And because they were willing, in unanimous and concerted action, to stake their lives on this truth. In a word, *such action becomes possible where fundamental truths are taken seriously.*[38]

Only those who have not experienced compassionate nonviolence can mistake it for passive inaction. Even some who work for peace may fall into the view that nonviolence is a passivity that does nothing and tolerates anything. Such "nonviolence of the weak" (as Gandhi called it[39]) easily degenerates into hidden forms of violence, the manifestation of ego-centered thoughts and actions dominated by fear or anger that seek peace and survival primarily for oneself or one's own race, nation, or religion.

37. Merton, *Nonviolent Alternative*, 213.
38. Ibid., 167.
39. Gandhi, *All Men Are Brothers*, 48.

In any case, violence is actually the expression of weakness and confusion. A weak man, inclined to violence, acts justly only by accident. It is the non-violent man (and, by extension, the non-violent society) which is consistently fair and just. Therefore a truly free and just society must be constructed on a foundation of non-violence.[40]

A nonviolent break in the cycle of our conditioned responses requires the development of understanding, compassion, and acceptance that we are all in this together. Christian nonviolence also involves a free and willing acceptance of suffering in the most positive and active manner. It embraces the dynamic spiritual force of divine love.

> The key to nonviolence is the willingness of the nonviolent resister to suffer a certain amount of accidental evil in order to bring about a change of mind in the oppressor and awaken him to personal openness and to dialogue.[41]

Thomas Merton did not believe that all violence on earth could be eliminated. However, he saw that each of us can become conscious of our habitual tendencies toward violence and self-centeredness, and that we can transform such habitual tendencies, thereby diminishing violence and suffering in ourselves and in the world.

> Conflict will never be abolished but a new way of solving it can become habitual.[42]

Merton understood that certain circumstances require physical force, a *protective* rather than *retributive* use of force. He did not think that anyone had to stand by as loved ones are harmed or killed. Indeed, Merton acknowledged the hypocrisy of advocating that people suffering under American economic and military violence should respond nonviolently.

> Instead of preaching the cross *for others* and advising them to suffer patiently the violence which we sweetly impose on them, with the aid of armies and police, we might

40. Gandhi, *Gandhi on Non-Violence*, 43.
41. Merton, *Nonviolent Alternative*, 217.
42. Ibid.

conceivably recognize the right of the less fortunate to use force and study more seriously the practice of non-violence and humane methods on our own part when, as it happens, we possess the most stupendous arsenal of power the world has ever known.[43]

Who are we to condemn a desperation we have helped to cause![44]

Merton also realized that by the mid-twentieth century the development of atomic, biological, and chemical weapons had made violence obsolete as a means of settling international conflicts. The catastrophic potential of these modern weapons clarifies that violence begets violence, making nonviolent Christian peacemaking the only alternative. One key to this peacemaking is the capacity for forgiveness. Forgiveness facilitates the creation of a present and future not scarred, determined, or undermined by the violence and errors of the past. Forgiveness facilitates peace by giving us room to be less victims of violence and more perpetuators of nonviolence.

To forgive others and to forget their offense is to enter with them into the healing mystery of death and resurrection in Christ, to return to the source of the Spirit which is the Heart of Christ. And by this forgiveness we are ourselves cleansed: *Unde vulneratus fueras, inde curare,* says Cyprian.[45]

In using violent force to end violence, we are engaging in attitudes and actions that are necessary to harm or kill other human beings, thereby cultivating a state of mind and a way of life that perpetuates suffering. Though violent action may appear to settle a conflict, it is always temporary and illusive. Nonviolence works not through destroying violence, but by accepting the reality of poverty and war and transforming it.

The reason for emphasizing non-violent resistance is this: he who resists force with force in order to seize power

43. Merton, *Nonviolent Alternative,* 190.

44. Ibid., 189.

45. Merton, "Gandhi," 18.

may become contaminated by the evil which he is resisting and, when he gains power, may be just as ruthless and unjust a tyrant as the one he has dethroned. A non-violent victory, while far more difficult to achieve, stands a better chance of curing the illness instead of contracting it. There is an essential difference here, for non-violence seeks to "win" not by destroying or even by humiliating the adversary, but by *convincing him* that there is a higher and more certain common good than can be attained by bombs and blood. Non-violence, ideally speaking, does not try to overcome the adversary by winning over him, but to turn him from an adversary into a collaborator by winning him over. Unfortunately, non-violent resistance as practiced by those who do not understand it and have not been trained in it, is often only a weak and veiled form of psychological aggression.[46]

Merton believed that realistic global disarmament and peace-making would have to involve the empowerment of a supranational organization like the United Nations to assist nations in resolving their conflicts with nonviolent means. Merton envisioned global peace and saw that such transformation would occur to the degree to which people in the United States and other economically and militarily powerful countries could relinquish their desires for global domination and profiteering, and embrace the greater goal of national and global health, human survival, and peace.

The only sane course that remains is to work frankly and without compromise for a supranational authority and for the total abolition of war.[47]

Merton suggests that when we take more interest in peace, then our actions will follow. He would likely be happy to know of the current movement among peace activists and members of the U.S. Congress to create a Department of Peace.[48]

46. Merton, *Faith and Violence*, 12–13.

47. Merton, *Nonviolent Alternative*, 120.

48. See the Web site of Americans for a Department of Peace (htp://www.af dop.org) or the Web site for Congressman Dennis Kucinich (http://www.kucin ich.house.gov/issues /issue//issue/?IssueID=1564).

> Can our government not divert some of the money paid
> out for our overkill capacity, to investigate the chances of
> lasting and realistic peace?[49]

Nonviolence requires us to accept that we will never become perfectly peaceful at all times within ourselves, or in our personal or international relationships. Furthermore, we need not wait until we are completely at peace within ourselves before we engage in social and political peacemaking. On the contrary, because the personal and political are interrelated phenomena, cultivating peace at any level of our life facilitates peace at all other levels as well. The peace in our hearts (or its absence) will shape our ability to be at peace and to help make peace at other levels of conflict.

Spiritual Growth

> The monk is committed to bringing about a human trans-
> formation that begins at the level of consciousness.[50]

Merton occasionally wrote about nonviolent peacemaking, but more often he discussed the process, or *psychology*, of transforming ourselves into people who know the compassion and love of Christ within. A Christian humanistic psychology of nonviolent peacemaking and spiritual growth centers on awareness and consciousness. We must begin our peacemaking wherever we are, because we cannot yet be any other place. As we become aware of our previously unconscious tendencies towards selfishness, we see how our ego-centered actions do not bring us peace and freedom. Through accepting what we become aware of, we simultaneously realize our own "higher" human potential to become like Christ.

> Therefore one of the most important tasks of the moment
> is to recognize the great problem of the mental climate
> in which we live. Our minds are filled with images which
> call for violent and erratic reactions. We can hardly re-
> cover our senses long enough to think calmly and make
> reasoned commitments.[51]

49. Merton, *Nonviolent Alternative*, 69.
50. Merton, *New Seeds of Contemplation*, 213.

One of the greatest impediments to nonviolent peacemaking is the desire to maximize personal pleasure, satisfaction, and comfort and avoid suffering and dissatisfaction. Merton realized that being tied to satisfying our personal desires makes us slaves to those desires, and he knew that we each have the ability to return to our free and peaceful true nature. One of the hallmarks of true Christian life (inside and outside of monasteries) is the willingness to accept the suffering that comes with not fulfilling our selfish desires.

> There can be no peace on earth without the kind of inner
> change that brings man back to his "right mind." [51]

Christian teachings refer to the process in which one's right mind is recovered as *metanoia, spiritual growth*. Other names for this are *repentance, conversion, enlightenment, salvation* or *liberation, spiritual warfare, spiritual peacemaking,* or *spiritual growth*. True spiritual growth—recovering one's right mind—is the source from which nonviolent peacemaking arises. Thinking clearly and coherently provides the antidote to ways of thinking that lead to violent actions.

We are in our right minds to the extent that we know ourselves to be children of God, and to the extent that we also know others to equally be children of God. We are in our right minds when love shapes our perceptions, when we respond to offenses with forgiveness, and when we make other aspects of nonviolent Christian peacemaking part of our spiritual practice and our human responses to today's violence. We can also know that we are in our right mind to the degree we take interest in understanding the experiences, concerns, and perspectives of others—even of those in conflict with us. Most important, we are in our right mind when we love God above all.

> The moral evil in the world is due to man's alienation
> from the deepest truth, from the springs of spiritual life
> within himself, to his alienation from God. [52]

Merton's "right mind" involves awareness of God within us and of a nonegocentric "hidden Self," a Divine gift with the potential to help us experience a sacred peace, fellowship, communion, and union with our Creator, who is at once within us and the ground

51. Merton, "Gandhi and the One-Eyed Giant," 20.
52. Merton, *Nonviolent Alternative*, 222.

of all being. A world of violence is a reflection and creation of those who live in it.

> The only way to change such a world is to change the thoughts and the desires of the men who live in it. The conditions of our world are simply an outward expression of our own thoughts and desires.[53]

Nonviolent Christian peacemaking involves awareness of both heart and mind. Our heart is our conscience, the place where the Holy Spirit communicates with each of us. Our clear and developed conscience leads us away from harming others or ourselves while it supports our ability to cultivate peace and love in life. Through self-awareness, we can discover who is keeping peace and love from us.

> What if we awaken to discover that *we* are the robbers, and our destruction comes from the root of hate in ourselves?[54]

To the extent we try to live as "individuals" (ego-centered or self-centered), we perpetuate the violence of separateness, alienation, illusion, and despair. Merton and Martin Luther King both said that the "individual" is an illusion created by the separating ego trying to make itself real and important. Merton said that when we "fall for" this illusion, our spiritual and psychological growth is stunted, and our actions will not support liberation, but violence.

> The supreme risk in this quest for liberation resides in the paradox of transcendence itself. For the Transcendent is also at the same time Immanent, and the mystery is that while man's spiritual liberation consists in a self-renunciation and self-recovery "beyond self," it is also at the same time a fantastic awakening to the truth and transcendent value of one's *ordinary self.*[55]

Spiritual and social transformation from violence to peace begins with awareness of our separation from our "ordinary" or "true" self, an awareness that serves to awaken us from an unconscious and

---

53. Merton, *Nonviolent Alternative*, 65.

54. Ibid.,186.

55. Merton, *Faith and Violence*, 114.

reactionary life. Transformation further evolves when we experience the true self directly. Indeed, the leap from knowing about love to experiencing it directly is crucial. We must set aside the ego-centered self to allow the love of Christ to be present within us.

> What we are asked to do at present . . . is not so much to speak of Christ as to let him live in us so that people may find him by feeling how he lives in us.[56]

This was Merton's last public statement before he died. He had questioned whether we would become aware, compassionate, courageous, and active enough to make peace, or whether we would destroy the world and ourselves before we could make such a global transformation. He wondered if the modern crises of poverty, war, and hunger would help awaken us to make peace, or if we were headed towards disaster.

> We are in the midst of what is perhaps the most crucial moral and spiritual crisis the human race has ever faced during its history. We are all deeply involved in this crisis, and consequently the way each [person] faces the crisis has a definite bearing on the survival of the whole race.[57]

Thomas Merton devoted a lifetime to inviting Christians to learn, practice, teach, and create in ways that acknowledge and appreciate the holiness of life. His work continues to challenge our organizations and traditions to learn, practice, and teach nonviolent peacemaking for the healing, growth and preservation of life.

56. Merton, quoted in Forest, *Living with Wisdom*, 216.
57. Merton, *Nonviolent Alternative*, 103.

7

Jim Douglass

JAMES WILSON Douglass was born on July 16, 1937, in Princeton, British Columbia, Canada. He grew up in Hedley, BC, a small mining town in the Rocky Mountains, where his father managed a gold mine. Douglass' Irish Catholic mother had prepared to become a Dominican sister prior to marrying his father, a widower with four children already in their teens.

James Douglass studied nuclear engineering at the University of California Berkeley, and English and philosophy at Santa Clara University. He did graduate work in English at the University of Kansas, and earned an MA in theology at the University of Notre Dame. Before being inspired to work for peace, Douglass intended to be a nuclear-weapons designer and was in the U.S. army in 1955 and 1956.

From 1962 to 1965, Douglass succeeded in persuading bishops at the Second Vatican Council to condemn total war and to support conscientious objection. He has also spent time in jails for his nonviolent civil disobedience, resisting U.S. nuclear and military policies. In the 1980s, he led efforts in tracking and protesting the U.S. Department of Energy's nuclear-weapons "White Train" that carried nuclear materials secretly, and in the 1990s he traveled to Iraq to noncooperate with the U.S.-led economic sanctions and wars against that country. Douglass and his wife, Shelley, together founded the Ground Zero Center for Nonviolent Action; the Agape Community, which tracked the White Train, and Mary's House, a Catholic Worker house in Birmingham, Alabama.

Douglass has written a series of four books on the theology of nonviolence: *The Non-Violent Cross* (1968), *Resistance and Contemplation* (1972), *Lightning East to West* (1983), and *The Nonviolent Coming of God* (1991). *The Nonviolent Coming of God* describes the ways Jesus of Nazareth embodied revolutionary nonviolence and taught it to the people of his day, who faced the choice between nonviolence and violent annihilation by the occupying Roman military forces. Jesus' prophecy that we all must choose between nonviolence and annihilation is no less true today than it was in his own time. In his writing, Douglass maintains that the resurrection of Jesus—the nonviolent coming of God—is still happening today in the form of worldwide revolutionary nonviolence.

Especially important are the connections Douglass makes between theological, psychological, political, and economic aspects of peacemaking and revolutionary nonviolence. In ways congruent with much of the best contemporary and traditional psychotherapies, he speaks as a seasoned social-change activist and theologian about human growth and potential. He presents a theology (logic of God) and a psychology (logic of the psyche) of nonviolent peacemaking, as well as of personal and social growth and transformation.

Douglass does not call on people of non-Christian traditions to become Christians, but he does call on Christians and all religious and spiritual people to become acquainted with the central aspects of nonviolent peacemaking that all religious and spiritual traditions contain. Douglass' writings and activism for social change have focused on nonviolent resistance to militarism, on noncooperation with injustice, and on compassionate witnessing to suffering as taught by Jesus and other religious teachers.

Teshuvah: Transformation Through Nonviolence

> The inconceivable change that occurred at Jesus' cross was that an empire's terrifying deterrent was transformed through the nonviolent resistance of love, truth and forgiveness.[1]

In his writings, Douglass highlights the peacemaking potential that comes from our becoming aware of the suffering caused by violence, and the peacemaking potential of our taking responsibility for creating violence and suffering. Finally, Douglass reveals the peacemaking potential of our compassionate resistance to violence and suffering.

1. Douglass, *Nonviolent Coming*, 145.

Douglass reminds us that the root meaning of the biblical word *teshuvah* is "turning."

> What does repentance from a nation's violence mean? To begin with, we know that the rabbinic word for repentance is *teshuvah,* "turning," a turning from sin to God, as derived from the biblical verb *shuv,* "to return." Its original meaning is a returning to God from *exile,* i.e., from that place of alienation/separation. Thus, *teshuvah* means returning to the path or way we have been given by the Creator, "the path at return from Exile, from Babylon (Babylon = the empires of this world)." Our violence has put us in exile in Babylon, the empire of violence.[2]

In "turning," each of us takes responsibility for the violence we contribute to (directly or indirectly, personally or politically), and we relinquish our connections and privileges that rely on such violence. Simultaneously, we take refuge in a higher calling of resisting war and economic violence through the power of love.

> *Teshuvah* means re-turning from the empire of violence to the nonviolent path of our Creator.[3]

Like Jesus, Douglass, along with Gandhi and Martin Luther King Jr., understands that nonviolence involves interrelated personal, social, and global transformations. More accurately, these transformations are aspects of a single transformation.

> The little-noticed basis of the entire Christian faith is that moment when faith moved the poor Jew, Jesus, living under the heel of an empire, to believe in the transforming power of the kingdom of God. Once that fire was ignited in Jesus, nothing on earth could extinguish his faith in the nonviolent coming of God, nor God's actual coming through that faith. No empire has ever had the power to stand against such faith. The British Empire had as little success with Jesus' Hindu successor, Gandhi, as the Roman Empire had with Jesus and the early Christians. The nonviolent coming of God is a growing force in

2. Douglass, *Nonviolent Coming,* 145.
3. Ibid., 145.

Humanity that will not be denied its full flowering in the world.[4]

One of Douglass' central themes is that this *teshuvah,* or nonviolent transformation, is already happening in our momentous age. Douglass writes that Jesus taught that the power of this transformation, which exists in each person, in every community, and in whole nations is much greater than we have realized, and that this transformation is the good news that Jesus offers.

> The good news is the story of resistance in communities all around the world. The people in the United States are a very small part of the world. Communities of nonviolent resistance exist all over the globe, and I believe that they are much more powerful in the long run than the United States government. That's the good news. The good news is also that people are willing to die for that.[5]

Douglass links the general resurrection, or the second coming of Jesus, to our willingness to suffer without retaliating and even to die for peace and justice. He also expresses this as the relaxing of attachment to ourselves and the strengthening of our concern for others; a sort of death of the old way and resurrection in turning to a new way.

> The good news is that there is a resurrection, but you have to die for that resurrection to occur in the people, in a wider sense. If we are willing to die, anything is possible. We are all going to have to die anyhow, so we might as well die the right way—for justice and peace, and for love.[6]

The combination of a willingness to suffer without responding violently while resisting injustice selflessly were central to Gandhi's nonviolent movement. Douglass illuminates the dynamic and transformative quality of this ability to accept suffering without retaliation as "active suffering."

---

4. Douglass, *Nonviolent Coming,* 58.

5. James Douglass. 2005. Interview by John Malkin. Audio recording. July 6. Free Radio Santa Cruz.

6. Ibid.

In response to Rome's power of annihilation, Jesus discovered at the heart of his people, in the deepening wisdom of the prophets, a way out which was in reality a way in. It was the way of nonviolent transformation, as first conceived by the nameless prophet of Second Isaiah in the collective Jewish experience of exile and suffering. The way of suffering, seen by Jesus in a different way in relation to God, was a way of hope. It was a new way of active suffering, which even Second Isaiah had not seen fully. Suffering the violence of Rome was to be turned around, to become a way of nonviolent change. It was to be seen not as God's punishment of the people, but as the people being called by God for the redemption of all peoples: "I will make you the light of the nations so that my salvation may reach the ends of the earth" (Is 49:6).[7]

The teaching of Jesus to "love your enemies" can be understood as a transformation of violence through active resistance and compassion. This "active suffering" is the hidden heart of nonviolent peacemaking.

For the people to become God's suffering servant was seen by Jesus not as passive but as active, initiated in resistance to evil as a way of overcoming evil through God's very being—Love of the Oppressor, Love of the Persecutor, Love of the Enemy as the hidden heart of Yahweh.

"Love your enemies and pray for those who persecute you; in this way you will be children of your loving God in heaven, who causes the sun to rise on bad people as well as good, and the rain to fall on honest and dishonest people alike" (Matt 5:44–45). One had to give way to the mystery of God and simply enter that mystery. One had to enter the new creation, the new humanity, the new reign of God.[8]

Douglass discusses the life and teachings of Jesus in terms of Jesus' resisting the Roman Empire of his day through the disciples' repenting of violence and turning to love. Jesus advocated a popular turning to compassion-based resistance and he warned of the destruction that would result if opposition to the empire turned violent.

7. Douglass, *Nonviolent Coming*, 83–84.
8. Ibid., 80–84.

Jesus is speaking collectively to his nation: "Unless you repent you will *all* likewise perish." Unless the nation repents by putting away its sword, it will perish by Rome's sword. There is an echo here consistent with Jesus' admonition in Matthew to the disciple who used his sword in Jesus' defense, cutting off the ear of the high priest's slave: "Put your sword back into its place; for all who take the sword will perish by the sword" (Mt 25:52).[9]

In recent years, Douglass has focused his research and writing on the nonviolent message and "turning" or transformation that connects the crucifixion of Jesus with the assassinations of Martin Luther King Jr., Malcolm X, John F. Kennedy and Robert F. Kennedy. The murders of these "two prophets, a president and a president-to-be," happened during a four-and-a-half-year span, between November 1963 and June 1968.

In June 1963 in his American University address, John F. Kennedy asked Americans to re-examine "our attitude towards the Soviet Union. . . . and the cold war" and the U.S. strategy of peacemaking through "American weapons of war." On October 2, 1963, Kennedy told his National Security Council advisors that he had decided to withdraw all U.S. troops from Vietnam by 1965. On November 22, 1963, he was assassinated.

> John F. Kennedy was murdered because he was turning, in the root biblical sense of the word "turning"—*teshuvah* in the Hebrew Scriptures, *metanoia* in the Greek, "repentance" in English. John Kennedy was murdered because as president of the United States he had begun to turn away from, to repent from, his own complicity with the worst of U.S. imperialism.[10]

Robert F. Kennedy planned to end the U.S. war in Vietnam as well as to investigate the assassination of his brother. He was killed only moments after winning the California Democratic primary on June 5, 1968, Douglass contends, not by a lone assassin but by a government that was threatened by the "turning" of this likely president-to-be.

9. Douglass, *Nonviolent Coming*, 145.
10. Douglass, "Letter to the American People."

> [Robert Kennedy was] turning away from, repenting
> from, his obedience to the same forces that had killed
> his brother. Turning away from military and corporate
> power. Turning toward the people.[11]

Before their assassinations, Martin Luther King Jr. and Malcolm
X were "turning" towards each other and finding common ground.
King was becoming more militant in his stand against the U.S. war
in Vietnam and was advocating a national strike through the Poor
People's Campaign. Malcolm X was playing a bigger role in the civil
rights movement and was traveling throughout Africa to cultivate an
international movement to confront the people and the government of
the United States regarding its treatment of African Americans.

> King was becoming more militant, and Malcolm was
> becoming much more a participant in the civil rights
> movement . . . [King] turned toward a very direct and
> dramatic resistance to the Vietnam War. That occurred
> one year to the day before his assassination, April 4,
> 1967, in his Riverside Church address. He was turning.
> He was being Malcolmized . . . And of course we all
> know about Malcolm's turn away from a very restrictive
> understanding of Islam in the Nation of Islam, to a much
> more profound understanding of Islam, just as King was
> experiencing a much more profound understanding of
> Jesus.[12]

Douglass points out that it took Martin Luther King Jr. a number
of years to oppose in public the U.S. war in Vietnam, and that when he
did, he lost privilege. The courage that King exemplified reminds us of
the selflessness and sacrifice required in nonviolent peacemaking.

> King said, "I can't preach nonviolence to these people
> [African Americans in U.S. ghettoes] anymore unless I
> can say, first of all, that my own government is the great-
> est purveyor of violence in the world today." And when
> he said that, he lost his privilege. He no longer was the
> friend of the president of the United States. He could no
> longer walk into the White House. He became a person

11. Douglass, "Letter to the American People."
12. Douglass, interview.

who was suddenly dropped from privilege. That is an example of how we need to speak and live the truth in such a way that we're not simply talking, but we need to walk some of the walk. Walk *all* of the talk for that matter.[13]

James Douglass writes from personal, firsthand experience of "turning" as well. His own interest in nuclear weapons began not when he became a social-change activist, but when he desired to design weapons for the U.S. government.

> I became aware of an emptiness in that experience that made it necessary for me just to turn around, almost literally, and leave the program, leave the University. I am not talking about a conversion to nonviolence. I enlisted in the United States army. But in the course of that process, I committed myself to speaking truth in a way that I really didn't understand. In the course of that, I wound up going to Santa Clara University and trying to understand what it meant to be a Catholic Christian rather than become a professional weapons designer, as I had started to be. I committed myself to seeking the truth, wherever it might lead me. In the course of that truth, a professor introduced me to Dorothy Day.[14]

Thanks to the resistance of Dorothy Day and the Catholic Worker communities, Douglass became aware of the compulsory civil-defense drills in New York City. The Catholic Workers' willingness to go to jail rather than to participate in the rehearsals for war inspired and challenged Douglass to confront the nuclear arms race and to work for peace. In 1958 he began writing for the Catholic Worker newspaper.

> Whether the Catholic Worker was working with the homeless, responding to the suffering of farm workers, injustice of U.S. policies in different parts of the world or the nuclear arms race, it was all in response to the teachings of Jesus in the Sermon on the Mount. And the Works of Mercy. It was all about peace. Step by step,

13. Douglass, interview.
14. Ibid.

I began to understand that the commitment of Jesus was to a totally nonviolent way.[15]

Resisting Institutional Violence: from the White Train to Iraq

He [Jesus] was definitely a nonviolent resister. He non-cooperated with and resisted evil on every possible level. There was nothing passive about Jesus any more than there was anything passive about Gandhi. And Gandhi, in his nonviolent resistance, even went to the point of saying that violent resistance was better than passivity. But he believed that there was always an alternative, which was the biggest priority on the scale, and that it is nonviolent resistance.

Douglass' peacemaking draws from the lessons of Jesus' life and teachings to address systemic (or institutional) violence. The example of Jesus' confronting the institutional violence in Jerusalem helps us today to address the violence we find in our own country's actions:

The logic of the use of violence to deter others from acts of conscience—and from the social revolution such acts add up to—comes from the assumption that systematic violence can dictate its own terms to anyone on the face of the earth. The systemic evils based on this assumption cover the globe. A systemic evil is a social organization of killing and injustice into which we become locked by co-ercion, propaganda, and our own passivity. Hiding death and lying about death head the agenda of any systemic evil. The first lie systemic evil forces us to accept is our obligation to believe its official lies about killing.[16]

Douglass points out that peacemaking requires taking responsibility for the ways that we pay for, cause, and otherwise perpetuate military, environmental, and other systemic violence. He also clari-

---

15. Douglass, interview.
16. Douglass, *Nonviolent Coming*, 21.

fies the way that threats of institutional violence deter individuals or groups from opposing those very institutions.

> Rome used to threaten entire cities with annihilation if the people resisted. That is not different than what our empire, the American empire, does today with nuclear weapons. Rome also threatened people individually with execution, with assassination. While they did it very publicly with crosses in squares and edges of town—centers of town, for that matter—we do the same. I think that the assassinations [of Martin Luther King Jr., et al.] that we were talking about a few minutes ago are examples. The people in power in the U.S.A. understand those examples.[17]

The Jews of Jesus' day were an occupied people suffering under and reacting to the violence of their Roman oppressors. The Roman army used the cross and the sword to punish rebels and to deter uprisings in order to maintain Roman privilege and power.

Douglass compares Rome's use of violence for deterring or putting down challenges to the U.S. government's threats of nuclear violence for deterring or putting down challenges to U.S. imperialism. Jesus warned his own people that they could choose annihilation or transformation, that they could resist the Romans with violence and be destroyed or resist nonviolently and create peace. Today we face the same options on a worldwide scale. In the case of Jerusalem and Rome, the people of Jerusalem turned to violence, and during the lifetime of many of Jesus' followers, Roman forces destroyed the entire city of Jerusalem.

> Unless we turn deeply, we, like our sisters and brothers in first-century Jerusalem, shall all likewise perish—all around the earth.[18]

In the 1980s Douglass' work to stop institutional violence addressed the nuclear weapons policies of the U.S. government. In 1982 Douglass and other activists became aware that the U.S. Department of Energy's White Train carried nuclear weapons and missile components to the Trident submarine base near Seattle, Washington.

---

17. Douglass, interview.
18. Douglass, *Nonviolent Coming*, 150.

Douglass and his wife, Shelley, bought a house next to the base and the train tracks. They cofounded the Agape Community to monitor the White Train.

> We decided to become the Agape Community and ad-opted a community statement which said in part: "We believe the spiritual force capable of both changing us and stopping the arms race is that of *agape*: the Love of God operating in the human heart." By this definition, we were basing our community especially on Martin Luther King's understanding of *agape*. As we tracked and opposed Trident missile propellant shipments through Utah, Idaho, Oregon, and Washington in 1981–82, two truths found a special life in the Agape Community. The first is that systemic evil shuns the light. The government and the railroads did their best to keep us from seeing the missile shipments. The second truth we experienced is that once evil is brought into the light, it can be over-come by God's love operating in our lives.[19]

Activists in 250 towns and cities in the United States formed a network along the nation's train tracks. Collectively they discovered the route of the White Train and the source of the nuclear weapons: the Pantex plant in Amarillo, Texas, assembled all the weapons from different component factories all over the country. Douglass recalls that the White Train, painted white on top for safety reasons was accompanied by rail security cars with a "high turret, like a tank's."[20] Hundreds of people were arrested along the tracks of the White Train, and in 1986 the U.S. government discontinued transporting nuclear weapons via train and began using trucks exclusively.[21]

> The guards in the White Train, the crews on Trident sub-marines, the thousands of missile technicians throughout the world who can plunge all of us into a river of fire, breathe with you and with me and with God. In that one breath of God is our hope of transformation.[22]

19. Douglass, *Nonviolent Coming*, 161–62.
20. Ibid., 62.
21. Ibid., 160.
22. Douglass, *Nonviolent Coming*, 85.

Douglass has traveled to Iraq four times to noncooperate with the U.S./U.N. sanctions against Iraq, and to deliver medicine and hospital supplies. The sanctions resulted in the deaths of five hundred thousand children under the age of five. In December 1994, Jim and Shelley Douglass supported Kathy Kelly and other activists who created Voices in the Wilderness, an organization dedicated to nonviolent noncooperation with the U.S./U.N. sanctions. In 1995 Douglass joined the first delegation to Iraq organized by Voices in the Wilderness. Most recently Jim Douglass was in Iraq with a Christian Peacemaker Team at the beginning of the second U.S. war on Iraq in March 2003.

> We went in during the first week of the war, through the front lines. Our purpose, of course, couldn't very well be to stop a war that had already begun. We hardly had that kind of power. We wanted simply to be in solidarity with the people under our bombs. We had done everything we could to try to keep that war from happening. As a Catholic, I went to Rome prior to the war and did everything I could to encourage the Pope—Pope John Paul II—to go to Iraq. He had taken a very strong stand against the war. I felt that if he went to Iraq, it might hold off, and even possibly prevent, that war. That didn't come about. So I felt that the last thing that I could do, and perhaps the only thing, was go to Iraq. We went with a wonderful community of people who all shared the commitment to nonviolence—the nonviolence of Jesus. We just went there to stand with the people of Iraq, under the bombs.[23]

In Iraq Douglass witnessed a remarkable real-life version of the Good Samaritan parable. He and the other members of the Christian Peacemaker Team were crossing the desert under the bombing of U.S. planes when one of the vans that his group was traveling in overturned after hitting a bomb crater in the road. A number of people were seriously injured in the accident.

> An Iraqi car came along, a group of Iraqis in it, and they saw this van off in the ravine and stopped their car, in the

23. Douglass, interview.

middle of this bombing, and went down and rescued the people. This is the parable of the good Iraqi, the parable of the good Samaritan retold in very vivid fashion, by the example of the Iraqis . . . In Rutba, a town where U.S. planes had just destroyed the hospital, a doctor from the hospital tended the wounds of our brothers in that car and literally saved their lives, in spite of the opposition of some of the people in the town who said, "How can you be doing this? Their country just bombed us." And he said, "We help everybody," and sent them on their way without charging a penny.[24]

Unfortunately the U.S. media never told the story of the good Iraqis. Another story that came out of Iraq on the same day grabbed the attention of the United States, playing instead on prejudices against the Iraqi people. This story was about the rescue of a U.S. soldier, Jessica Lynch, who had reportedly been tortured by Iraqis in a hospital. Later the facts of the story were disputed, and it was revealed that Lynch had not been tortured. The media's choice of which story to highlight—either the compassionate story of "loving your enemy" or the story of the "enemy" as evil—provides a vivid example of one way that "media violence" (in this case, violence that the media inflicts upon the public through news selection and suppression) regularly manifests itself.

Jesus Taught Human Equality

Douglass makes clear that the teaching of Jesus points toward equality for men and women, for the rich and the poor, for Jews and Gentiles, for blacks and whites. An essential awareness of the non-violent kingdom of God is that *everyone* needs freedom, love, and peace. Understanding these needs affects the deepest psychological, spiritual, and political levels of our lives. Douglass asserts that Jesus used the inclusive phrase "father and mother" in the Lord's Prayer.

The nuances of Jesus' teaching, from love of enemies to parables of compassion, bring us to understand that the prayer he taught the disciples began, in essence, "Abba-Ima" ("Papa-Mama"). What profound effect would have

24. Douglass, interview.

followed had the church recognized from the very beginning this dimension of Jesus' teaching, by expressing the
first line of the Lord's Prayer as "Our Abba-Ima who is
in heaven"?[25]

Douglass also points out that some of Jesus' female followers
had more faith in him and in his nonviolent teachings than did many
of his male followers.

> Whereas the male disciples despaired and fled in terror
> from Jesus' execution, many of the women disciples
> stayed to witness Jesus' death: Mary of Magdala, Mary
> who was the mother of James and, Salome, and "many
> other women who had come up to Jerusalem with him"
> (Mark 15:40–41). In a striking demonstration of the
> New Humanity, a group of these women had been dis-
> ciples of Jesus ever since Galilee (Luke 8:1–3). Contrary
> to every dictate of their society concerning women, they
> had remained with Jesus all the way to Jerusalem. In the
> final events that shattered and dispersed the male dis-
> ciples, this core group of women continued, in spite of
> their fear, to "look on from afar" (Mark 15:40).[26]

These examples remind us to reexamine our attitudes towards
gender discrimination in religion and society and to embrace the
female and male aspects that create wholeness in each of us.

A key component that helps us to "love our enemies" is the
understanding that each person holds a piece of the truth. This is
another way of saying that we all are part of a whole, that our lives
are "inextricably linked," as Martin Luther King Jr. said, and that our
thoughts and actions affect others. By accepting that someone with
whom we disagree is acting in the truth that they best understand,
we are practicing a form of radical love and nonviolence, a method
for building understanding and connection between people.

> With regard to the war on terrorism, I believe that there
> should be something we can find of truth in Osama bin
> Laden or Mr. Bush, depending on whom we feel a deepest
> conflict with. I say that one needs to examine the truth

25. Douglass, *Nonviolent Coming*, 105–6.
26. Ibid., 58.

coming from both of them. I think that Osama bin Laden, and all those whom we identify as terrorists, just as all those whom we identified as communists thirty years ago, are responding to incredible suffering caused, to a large degree, from policies by our own government . . . I will look anywhere for agreement with somebody. What are the bridges to that person? As hard as it is to find a bridge, I will look for it. I think that is the position of Gandhi, and the position that we need to seek out and embrace if we are going to have a peaceful and just world.[27]

When we believe that we can find peace by identifying and eliminating our enemies, we are cultivating violence. Through our "enemies," however, we can realize the kingdom of God. There is no way to create a peaceful community other than by being at peace. And this requires the task of realizing the presence of God in all, especially in our "enemies."

"Love your enemies" means to realize the presence of God through our enemies. In the historical alternatives we and Jerusalem are given, not to realize the presence of the kingdom of God through our enemies is to choose death. We begin to choose death as soon as we place the kingdom of God at a distance and yearn for the means of getting there, as every violent revolution has done. Set at a distance, the kingdom as end will justify any means on earth, beginning with the killing of our enemies, those same enemies who right now represent the possibility of God's kingdom. To kill our enemies is to kill the presence of the kingdom.[28]

In part Jesus taught that resistance includes resistance to despair and fear. If we think that our actions will not make a difference in the world, then we are not likely to work towards peace and justice. Those who own the wealth and resources encourage such despair as a strategy for disempowering those who are striving for economic and social justice. We can sink into such despair if we believe that

27. Douglass, interview.
28. Douglass, *Nonviolent Coming*, 162.

we should see immediate results from our efforts to change ourselves and the world around us.

> Our rulers will allow us to do virtually anything that we want in protest to their rule just so long as we do not overcome our despair as a people.[29]

The Church Obscures Jesus' Teachings

The historical consequences of the early church's obscuring of Jesus' prophecy of nonviolent transformation have been momentous . . . The most critical shift can be seen in the layers of tradition in the synoptic gospels themselves, from Jesus' own eschatology of nonviolence to Mark's, Luke's, and Matthew's mixed messages.[30]

Douglass has detailed how the church has obscured or opposed the teachings of Jesus. In the fourth century, the political power of the day, Rome, came together with the religious power of the day, the Catholic Church, and began to use the teachings of Jesus to protect the wealthy minority. Douglass and other Christian peacemakers believe that much of the Catholic Church accepts and perpetuates some forms of violence—violence based on what pacifist theologians like Walter Wink call the "Constantinian heresy," whereby church and state use Jesus' teachings to validate military violence.[31]

The power of nonviolence is so strong that governments have often educated their citizenry to believe that Jesus' teachings on love, compassion, patience, forgiveness, and nonviolence are conditional, impractical, and best viewed as historical narrative. Christians who have wanted to avoid the likely consequences of obstructing systems of violence have often framed biblical interpretations to correspond with those institutions currently holding power through the threat or use of violence. Douglass points to the importance of recalling that Jesus' teachings were offered within a context of systemic, state-sponsored violence.

29. Douglass, "Letter to the American People," 5.
30. Douglass, *Nonviolent Coming*, 181.
31. Lasserre, *War and the Gospel*, 195.

Rome's deterrent policy was understood by Jesus to risk the destruction of the current Jewish world, an event which was in fact to occur in 70 C.E. Rome, like the United States, used an escalating threat to deter colonized peoples.[32]

When Christian leaders and congregations allow war makers to use the teachings of Jesus to support violence, then "love your enemies" quickly becomes "love your enemies only if they love you," and "love your neighbors as yourself" is understood as "love your neighbors as yourself unless you are angry at them." Douglass beckons us to question the relationship between the church and the violence of the state.

> Jesus, as we all know when we think about it, wasn't a Christian. He was a Jew. And Christianity as we know it today, to a large extent, derives from a church—the church I belong to, the Catholic Church—allying itself to Constantine. From the fourth century on, the Catholic Church and Christianity have become deeply involved in an empire that has been succeeded by a number of other empires, including the American empire that we have today.[33]

The early followers of Jesus called themselves simply, "the Way." Even the power of the Roman Empire could not stop them. Though often obscured and used to justify violence, Jesus' essential teachings on transforming love have been passed down through generations.

> I think that the best followers of Jesus, the best exponents of his teaching, are probably not Christian. Because we have too much propaganda involved in Christianity, and too much of another empire that calls itself Christian in many of its propaganda issuances and statements . . . Jesus is moving in a different direction from Christianity from the very beginning. Gandhi is the greatest exemplar of the teachings of Jesus, and Gandhi, of course, was not a Christian. That says something, from the very beginning, about how we might understand Jesus' teachings. They are

32. Lasserre, *War and the Gospel*, 15.
33. Douglass, interview.

in profound conflict with the way in which Christianity has developed. Especially the way that it exists today.[34]

Douglass also writes interpretations of the Gospels. In *The Nonviolent Coming of God*, Douglass considers the teachings of Jesus and the different ways that they have been understood. Many contemporary Christians believe that Jesus' warning of the "end of the world" was a prophecy of annihilation through war and environmental devastation. Douglass argues that Jesus was actually reminding those who would listen that their own actions would lead either to annihilation or liberation; violent opposition would lead to annihilation, but the nonviolent alternative would lead to freedom. On another level, Jesus was also striving toward, and predicting, an "end of the world" *as it was*; an end to the economic and military oppression of the Roman Empire. Likewise, Douglass understands the general resurrection and second coming of Jesus to be the birth of this nonviolent way of life, based in love, compassion, and equality.

> Jesus had two basic ways of envisioning the alternative to the kind of destruction that war and violence of every kind has brought in the world. He talked about the kingdom, or reign, of God, which was his vision of an "upside down" kingdom. It is a kingdom where the poorest and the most oppressed are first . . . That is true in his parables; it is true in his teachings. It is true in how he lived and how he died—crucified by the empire.[35]

Douglass emphasizes that in the Gospels, Jesus always refers to himself with the Aramaic phrase *bar enasha*. Often translated as "son of man," the phrase actually means "the human being." Jesus was saying; "I am humanity," because he saw liberation—the Kingdom of God—coming through a collective human transformation. "Those who took the sword would perish by the sword."

> At the heart of Gandhi's satyagraha, and of Jesus' "Kingdom of God" and "the Human Being," is an infinite force of transformation: the nonviolent power to change violence and oppression into community, the soul-based

34. Douglass, interview.
35. Ibid.

power to realize unity progressively in a person, a society, and a world. That transformation and realization is occurring in the remarkable time in which we live.[36]

According to Douglass, the nonviolent second coming of Jesus is happening now, in the form of compassionate action. In embracing suffering rather than trying to destroy or ignore it, and in opposing systems of violence through soul-force, we "human beings" cooperate in the resurrection and the kingdom of God.

> Jesus' second coming, as we have been led to believe, could be . . . on a nuclear cloud. On the contrary, the way it is expressed in the Gospels is that it would be totally consistent with his first coming, which was as a person who was born into poverty and who lived with the poor and died with the poor. So that Jesus' coming in the world is a nonviolent coming.[37]

Jesus taught that if we choose it, the kingdom of God is within our power in the present moment. The kingdom of God, like peace itself, is not something to encounter after we die, but is available now.

> The only way that nonviolence goes anywhere is if it is lived, and if it involves risk and solidarity. And identifying with people who are in positions quite different than a number of us who live in North America especially.[38]

36. Douglass, *Nonviolent Coming*, 31.
37. Douglass, interview.
38. Ibid.

8

Kathy Kelly

Kathy Kelly, a beacon of compassion and nonviolent action, has served the poor, comforted the wounded, and led international efforts to noncooperate with systems of violence. She has helped to bring attention to past and present destruction caused by the U.S. wars and economic sanctions against Iraq.

Kelly's parents met in London in 1944 during bombing by the Luftwaffe. Her Irish American father, Frank, was an American soldier. Before joining the military, he had spent half his life in the Christian Brothers religious congregation. Kelly's mother, Catherine, born to an indentured servant in Ireland, later worked in a children's hospital in England. After Kelly's father was hospitalized in 1993 with severe depression, she became his main caregiver until he died in 2000.

Kathy Kelly, one of six children, was born on December 10, 1952 on the southwest side of Chicago, where racial tensions ran high. She attended St. Paul-Kennedy, a "shared time" high school that combined classes between two schools a block apart: a private Catholic school, St. Paul, and a public school, Kennedy. Sometimes, police with dogs patrolled the halls of Kennedy, where fights between black and white students broke out regularly. During classes one day, white football players ran down the hallway screaming, "Kill the n—!" Kathy's teacher responded by closing the door and finishing the work on the blackboard.

> I had a lump in my throat and couldn't see the blackboard through my tears, but there was no way, at that point, that I would have raised my hand or my voice.[1]

---

1. Kelly, *Other Lands Have Dreams*, 14.

Kathy Kelly has devoted her adult life to raising her voice and dedicating her mind and body to standing up against injustice and making peace based on the teachings and life of Jesus. After studying the Nazi Holocaust, she realized the importance of moving from spectator to peacemaker.

> At a deep emotional level, I never wanted to be a spectator, a bystander, sitting on my hands or standing on the sidelines in the face of unspeakable evil.[2]

At school Kelly studied Martin Luther King Jr. and his summons that "Christians must be ready to bet their lives on their beliefs."[3] She also learned about Daniel Berrigan, a Catholic priest who had resisted the Vietnam War and nuclear-weapons deployment. She wondered what it would take to follow in the footsteps of these peacemakers, to give over and risk her life for peacemaking. The writings of William Stringfellow, author of An Ethic for Christians and Other Strangers in an Alien Land, inspired her further. A lawyer and Episcopal minister who had worked in Harlem, Stringfellow presented a scriptural analysis that pointed to "radical activism." Kelly also found role models in the nuns at her Catholic high school.

> The nuns shared everything. They lived in very simple conditions. What surprises me is not so much that I wanted, eventually, later in my life, to recapture some of those ideals, but that more people haven't sensed that there is a certain wisdom to sharing resources and living more simply and sharing income and being able to collectivize the shared wealth and make that available to other people who don't have as much.[4]

Kelly received a BA from Loyola University at Chicago in 1974 and later received a masters in religious education at the Chicago Theological Seminary. She has taught in Chicago-area community colleges and high schools since 1974. During her graduate studies, merely writing papers about poverty frustrated her, so in 1977 she

2. Kelly, *Other Lands Have Dreams*, 15.

3. Ibid., 18.

4. Kelly, interview.

moved to Uptown, the Chicago neighborhood where the Francis of
Assisi Catholic Worker House sponsored a soup kitchen and shelter.

> New friends in Uptown lived out the values that I'd been
> extolling in papers and exhorting in classrooms, and the col-
> lective determination to form a community that included
> street people, shut-ins, new immigrants, and whomsoever
> knocked on the door of the local Catholic Worker House
> was purely exhilarating and often tremendous fun.[5]

Later she met Roy Bourgeois, a Maryknoll priest who was leading Christian-based protests against the U.S-funded death squads
in Central America during the 1980s and Bourgeois later organized
protests at the School of the Americas. Kelly then met activist Karl
Meyer, who challenged her to take part in nonviolent direct actions
protesting draft registration. (She was married to Karl Meyer from
1982 to 1994.) For the first of many times, Kelly was arrested for
peacemaking actions.

> He helped me understand that one of the greatest gifts
> in life is to find a few beliefs that you can declare with
> passion and then have the freedom to act on them. For
> me, those beliefs are quite simple; that nonviolence and
> pacifism can change the world, that the poor should be
> society's highest priority, that people should love their
> enemies, and that actions should follow conviction, re-
> gardless of inconvenience.[6]

In 1985 Kelly received a grant from the Jesuits that enabled
her to visit Nicaragua. There she met Miguel D'Escoto, a Maryknoll
Catholic priest who served as the Foreign Minister.

> D'Escoto spent much of the evening outlining his plan
> to begin a lengthy fast "for peace, in defense of life, and
> against contra violence." He spoke at length about the
> cross, emphasizing that we must be willing to accept
> change and death. Then he talked about his confidence
> in the potential of Christians to make a difference, em-
> phasizing that new ways and means must be tried. He

---

5. Kelly, *Other Lands Have Dreams*, 17.
6. Ibid., 17.

spoke gently about nonviolence, his long, deep admira-
tion for Rev. Dr. Martin Luther King, Jr., and his clear
belief that Christians must be ready to bet their lives on
their beliefs.[7]

Soon thereafter Kelly decided to devote all her time to opposing
the U.S. military actions in Central America. In 1986 she resigned
midsemester from her teaching position at St. Ignatius College Prep
High School.

> In a letter to the students and faculty, I wrote, "As many
> of you know, I spent seven weeks in Nicaragua this sum-
> mer . . . As a result of all that I have seen and heard, I
> have reached a strong conviction that the United States
> is doing a terrible and evil thing in financing the contra
> attacks against Nicaragua." I explained that I was quit-
> ting my job to devote myself full time to opposing contra
> aid and that I found it intolerable to be comfortable at
> liberty in a country where people will stand by or accede
> to crimes against the life of another people.[8]

Kathy Kelly has edited and contributed to a number of books
and is the author of a collection of essays and stories titled *Other
Lands Have Dreams: From Baghdad to Pekin Prison* (Counterpunch,
AK Press, 2005). She wrote the book mostly in hotels in Iraq and
Jordan, and in U.S. prisons and jails. She has also been published in
a variety of journals, including the *National Catholic Reporter*, the
*Columbia Journal of International Affairs, Fellowship of Reconciliation
Magazine*, and *Yes Magazine*. Kelly has received numerous awards
for her work, including the 1998 Pax Christi Teacher of Peace Award
and the 2003 Thomas Merton Center Award. She has been nomi-
nated three times for the Nobel Peace Prize: in 2000 (with Dennis
Halliday) and in 2001 and 2003 (with Voices in the Wilderness).

7. Kelly, *Other Lands Have Dreams*, 18.
8. Ibid., 19.

Nonviolent Direct Actions

> I think it is very important to use, as the laboratory
> for nonviolence, our everyday experience. Take time to
> mine from that experience. What can we learn about
> ourselves, about our own propensity for violence?[9]

The nonviolence of Jesus involves an intertwined personal and collective transformation. To the extent that Kathy Kelly has taken responsibility for and transformed her own propensity for violence through the power of compassion, her ability to witness, resist and noncooperate with the suffering of war and poverty have expanded.

She has been arrested numerous times for a variety of nonviolent direct actions. Kelly has protested draft registration, participated in sit-ins and die-ins, five times has planted corn on nuclear missile silos, protested Project ELF and the testing of nuclear weapons by France, spoke out during Madeline Albright's appointment as Secretary of State and interrupted Albright's talk at the Chicago Council on Foreign Relations, opposed Clinton's 1993 bombing of Iraq, and blocked U.S. troops bound for Honduras.

In 1988 Kelly and thirteen others carried out simultaneous direct actions as part of the Missouri Peace Planting; a project to sow corn on many of the one hundred fifty missile silos that surrounded Kansas City. She was later sentenced for the action and served nine months in the Lexington, Kentucky, maximum-security prison.

In April of 2002, Kelly was among the first internationals to visit the Jenin refugee camp in the occupied West Bank after fighting between Israeli Defense Forces (IDF) and Palestinians left at least fifty-four Palestinians and twenty-four IDF soldiers dead. Kelly has also helped to organize and participated in nonviolent direct action teams in Iraq (1991), Bosnia (1992 and 1993), and Haiti (summer of 1994).

> Had our team, which lived in a small town in the southern finger of Haiti, been copied one hundred times over, throughout Haiti, I think the violence being wreaked on Haitian people could have been diminished. I was only there for three months, but others who were there for

9. Kelly, interview, 17.

a longer stay recorded the Haitian commandant saying: "I am ashamed and embarrassed that it was left to the foreigners on the hill to preserve the peace and security of this region."[10]

In an effort to further noncooperate with violent institutions and deny financial support to U.S. war makers, Kelly has refused to pay all federal income tax for the past twenty-four years. She joins the long history of nonviolent Christian peacemakers in the United States who have engaged in war-tax resistance.

> One of the most important "spiritual directors" in my life has been the Internal Revenue Service. Janis Joplin's lyric, "Freedom's just another word for nothing left to lose," comes to mind. War tax refusers learn ways to become impervious to collection, and that generally means finding ways to live without owning property, relying on savings, or growing attached to a job that one couldn't leave in the event of an IRS notice about wage garnishment.[11]

In 1987 Kelly was working at Prologue High School, which had fifty members of rival gangs as students, and where at least three students had died in gang violence during the year. During this time, realizing more clearly the connection between the ever-increasing U.S. military budget and the dwindling funds for education, Kelly decided to take more direct action against institutions that perpetuate violence and injustice.

> I knew that I couldn't continue my work without taking a stronger stand against policies that allotted billions of dollars towards weapons buildup while young people in blighted urban areas could barely survive their teen years.[12]

On January 17, 1991, a United States-led coalition launched a war against Iraq in response to that country's August 2, 1990, invasion of Kuwait. Though the war officially ended in February, it continued via the most intense economic sanctions ever imposed against

10. Kelly, *Other Lands Have Dreams*, 25.

11. Ibid., 18.

12. Ibid., 21.

a country. Kelly joined the Gulf Peace Team encampment on the Iraqi side of the Iraqi-Saudi border and remained at the border for the first fourteen days of the 1991 air war against Iraq. Iraqi officials then evacuated the group to the Al Rashid Hotel in Baghdad. After a bomb struck nearby, the team evacuated again to Jordan, where Kelly stayed for six months to help coordinate medical-relief convoys.

Voices In The Wilderness

In 1995 several activists who had been to Iraq before, during, and after the first Gulf War met in Kathy Kelly's Chicago apartment to create a nonviolent challenge to the U.S./U.N. economic sanctions against Iraq. On January 15, 1996, the newly formed organization, Voices in the Wilderness (VITW), sent a letter to then-U.S. Attorney General Janet Reno stating that they would break the sanctions as often as possible to bring medical-relief supplies and medicines to Iraq. The U.S. Treasury Department warned that if the group carried out its mission, members would risk twelve years in prison and a one million dollar fine. VITW has organized seventy delegations to Iraq, and Kelly has accompanied them twenty-seven times since 1996, delivering medicine in violation of the U.S./U.N. sanctions.

On August 12, 2005, a U.S. federal district court judge ordered Voices in the Wilderness to pay a $20,000 fine for bringing medicine to Iraq during the U.S./U.N. sanctions. VITW responded, "We choose to continue our noncooperation with the government's war on the Iraqi people through the simple act of refusing to pay this fine. To pay the fine would be to collaborate with the U.S. government's ongoing war against Iraq. We will not collaborate."[13]

During her many visits to Iraq, Kelly saw that twelve years of U.S./U.N. sanctions resulted in the death of thousands of children. The United Nations reported in 1999 that half a million Iraqi children had died as a result of ten years of sanctions. On May 12, 1996, CBS correspondent Lesley Stahl interviewed then-U.S. Ambassador to the United Nations (later U.S. Secretary of State) Madeleine Albright: "More than 500,000 Iraqi children are already dead as a result of the U.N. sanctions. Do you think the price is worth paying?"

13. Voices in the Wilderness. "Federal Judge Orders Fine Against US Citizens for Bringing Medicine to Iraq," press release, August 14, 2005.

Albright responded, "This is a very hard choice. But, yes, we think the price is worth it."[14] In 1998 and 2000 respectively, UN humanitarian coordinators for Iraq, Denis Halliday, and Hans von Sponeck, resigned in protest against the sanctions. Kathy Kelly and Voices in the Wilderness continue to follow the example of Jesus in caring for children and in nonviolently opposing institutions that endanger young lives.

> Jesus lived at a time when babies were very, very precarious in their lives. There were throwaway children all of the time. If a woman gave birth to a baby girl, the husband might say, "Throw it out, and let's try again." Jesus said, "Let the little ones come unto me." The little children that nobody seemed to be looking out for. And I have had that experience, too, where hordes of kids in a poor neighborhood in Haiti or Iraq will come running over and you're tripping over them. Jesus was very clear. He said, "Let these children stay with me." There aren't any throw-away people. There is a great amount to be learned from examining how we honestly treat our young people.[15]

In March 2003 Kelly again maintained a presence in Baghdad with the Iraqi Peace Team throughout the bombardment and invasion. In an effort to stand beside those who are suffering, the peace team witnessed the "shock-and-awe" bombing of Baghdad, designed to traumatize the civilian population.

> As I write, I can hear explosions in the distance. Clouds of smoke are billowing in every direction. We've heard that last night's casualty list includes 207 wounded, four of whom died in hospitals. News reports say that more than 1,000 Cruise missiles were launched last night, and the U.S. may be planning to release many more tonight. On a beautiful spring day, welcome to hell. (March 22, 2003)[16]

By accepting the suffering of the bombing and extending compassion to the Iraqis on the receiving end of the attack, Kelly has

14. Albright, Madeleine, interview by Lesley Stahl, *60 Minutes*, CBS, May 12, 1996.

15. Kelly, interview, 27.

16. Kelly, *Other Lands Have Dreams*, 66.

taken responsibility for the reality of the violence and has worked to make peace during war.

> I felt dismay, sadness, anger—but also a familiar sense of intense determination not to let the bombs have the last word.[17]

When U.S. troops arrived in Baghdad on a military occupation that continues to this day, Kelly and others greeted them with banners hanging from their hotel balcony that read, "Courage for Peace Not For War," "War = Terror," and "Life is Sacred." They offered the tired, thirsty soldiers water and fresh dates, and listened to their stories about crossing the desert and about the suffering of war. In April 2003 Kelly wrote about one of the first car bombings in Iraq against U.S. soldiers. Since then, car bombings occur daily in and around Baghdad. Since the March 2003 "shock-and-awe" attacks, estimates of the number of Iraqis killed in the invasion and occupation range from 83,000 to 655,000.[18] As of November, 2007, the number of U.S. troops killed in Iraq is estimated at 3,855.[19]

> I feel ready to insist with passion that war is never an answer.[20]

Since 2003 Kelly has returned to Iraq twice, for seventeen-day visits with team members who've remained in Baghdad. She has dedicated her book, *Other Lands Have Dreams,* to the children of Iraq.

Jesus: "Love Your Enemies"

> I believe that it is important to lovingly accept people where they are. And to try to continually practice as much intellectual honesty as we can for where we ourselves are.[21]

17. Kelly, *Other Lands Have Dreams*, 60.

18. The figure 83,000 comes from "Iraq Body Count" (http://www.iraqbody count.org) in November 2007. The number 655,000 comes from Burnham, Lafta, et al., "Mortality after the 2003 Invasion of Iraq."

19. Associated Press, "2007 Becomes Deadliest Yet for U.S. in Iraq."

20. Kelly, *Other Lands Have Dreams*, 63.

21. Kelly, interview, 10.

Throughout her peacemaking efforts, Kathy Kelly has cultivated an ability to notice the good heart in all people, often in circumstances where she may disagree with their ideas or actions. This practice of "loving one's enemy" transforms violence into peace, and transforms enemies into human beings worthy of sympathy. In her essays about being arrested for civil disobedience and nonviolent direct actions, Kelly describes being interrogated, being held at gunpoint, and being physically hurt. Yet from these experiences she emphasizes those moments when a soldier or law-enforcement officer showed her kindness and understanding.

One such experience occurred on August 15, 1988. Kelly and thirteen other social-change activists had climbed barbed wire fences enclosing some of the 150 missile silos that surrounded Kansas City, Missouri, to plant corn on the silos. Soon after she planted five kernels of bright pink corn and hung two banners saying, "Disarm and Live" and "You Can't Hug A Child With Nuclear Arms," three soldiers arrived in a jeep. They handcuffed Kelly and told her to kneel down. Two soldiers left, and the remaining one stood behind her, his gun pointed at her back. Kelly began to tell the soldier why she had taken this action and about the relationship between domestic poverty and the cost of nuclear weapons. When she asked the soldier if he wanted to pray, and he answered, "Yes, ma'am," Kelly recited the "Peace Prayer" of Saint Francis. The soldier then offered her a drink of water, asking her to tip her head back.

> He must have used both hands to give me that drink of water. We didn't disarm the nuclear missile silo sites of Missouri that morning, but one soldier took a risk and put down his gun to perform an act of kindness for a perfect stranger.[22]

On another occasion, November 23, 2003, almost fourteen thousand protestors gathered at Fort Benning, Georgia, the site of the Western Hemisphere Institute for Security, formerly called the School of the Americas. Peace activists oppose the institute for training military and law-enforcement personnel of other countries in techniques of terror and torture. Kelly was among twenty-seven activists arrested for trespassing, a crime for which she spent three

22. Kelly, *Other Lands Have Dreams*, 23.

months in Pekin Federal Prison Camp. During her arrest, a female military police officer "womanhandled" Kelly, subjecting her to an aggressive body search. Kelly was "hogtied" (her wrists and ankles were cuffed and then bound together), and then she was kneed in the back. But, again, she emphasizes only a gesture of understanding and kindness that she experienced.

> It's important to note . . . that one of the soldiers treated me kindly . . . he gently squeezed my shoulder. I won't forget that.[23]

By entering war zones and other places of great suffering to transform anger into love, Kathy Kelly brings to life the teaching of Jesus to "love your enemy." This Christian nonviolence affects not only those directly involved, but also can transform those who observe from a distance the power of compassion in response to violence.

> The key of nonviolence is control. It is natural to feel anger. That is just not going to go away. But if you can control the energy of that anger—learn not to react—than you have a chance to not only express loving care toward the opponent, but to affect the point of view of the onlooker. That is what we learned from the civil rights movement. Eventually the onlookers had a choice between identifying with Bull Connor, as he sprayed fire hoses on children, or the civil rights activists that were willing to take the blows themselves.[24]

Taking Responsibility

Kathy Kelly reminds us to acknowledge the progress that movements for peace and justice have achieved in the United States, including the abolishing of slavery, the ensuring of women's right to vote, and the increasing of labor rights and civil rights. The peace movements also remind us to use the power of love that Jesus taught, to acknowledge the suffering and violence that run through our history (including the slavery of half a million Africans), the genocide of the native population, nuclear war, and international militarism.

23. Kelly, *Other Lands Have Dreams*, 139.
24. Kelly, interview, 17.

The U.S. must come to grips with having been, since World War II (when under the shadow of the mushroom cloud we ushered the world into the nuclear age), a nation constantly at war: Korea, Vietnam, Nicaragua, El Salvador, Grenada, Panama, the first Gulf War, Kosovo, Colombia, Afghanistan, the ongoing war in Iraq.[25]

Kelly believes that we must view the terrorist attacks of September 11, 2001, as part of the previous conflicts and violence that the United States itself has instigated. She suggests our taking responsibility and cultivating understanding as a strategy to reconcile conflicts and to eliminate terrorism.

Why do some people in the Islamic world hate us so much? It's a quick discussion. We take over and dominate other people's societies. We set up client states in their regions and rely on these client states to house U.S. bases. We foster double standards, condemning invasion and occupation when it suits us (e.g., the Iraqi invasion of Kuwait) and yet undertaking or supporting murderous sanctions, invasions, and occupations, while claiming to support and enhance democratic states. Hideous and violent terrorist attacks will continue as long as we insist on taking other people's precious and irreplaceable resources for cut-rate prices.[26]

We can take a step in taking responsibility for violence, a step toward reducing war and hatred, by confronting the present financial priorities of our government, which include a 2005 military and security budget of $524 billion.[27]

There's no way to run or hide from the truth of the U.S. people's responsibility for reckless warfare, military and economic, in numerous parts of the world. Nor can we hide from the truth about who pays to prepare for future wars. In next year's defense budget [2006], $177 billion

---

25. Kelly, *Other Lands Have Dreams*, 102.
26. Ibid., 146.
27. Ibid., 14.

is earmarked for weapon systems that won't be available until two generations from now.[28]

In becoming aware of the ways we contribute to personal and collective violence, we can discover ways to cultivate personal and collective transformation by liberating ourselves from the fear and anger that lead to violence. Kelly and other Christian peacemakers challenge the belief that we can realize a peaceful world—the kingdom of God—only after this life and only after the physical annihilation of the world.

> Jesus said, "I have come to preach good news to the poor, liberty to the captives, release for the oppressed and to proclaim the acceptable year of the Lord" [cf. Luke 4:18–20]. That acceptable year had everything to do with distributing the resources and making sure that nobody was left out. That is quite a challenge and as far as I can tell, it has very little to do with being suddenly absorbed up into heaven by a vacuum cleaner with the rapture! I think there is plenty of guideline, plenty of prophecy, if you will, that points to a world in which it is easier to be good. And a way forward in which we can create a new world within the shell of the old.[29]

The more access we have to resources and comfort, the more responsibility we share to help alleviate the suffering of others. Kathy Kelly realized this anew upon her release from Pekin Prison.

> I think of another line from scripture; "To whom much is given, much is expected." Now that I have got my freedom back, there is a lot that is expected of me. I cannot rest with the idea that there is a deity that wants any prison in this country to continue for one more day. Not when you have leaders of major faith-based communities in our world clamoring for compassion and love of enemy and respect for all human beings. You don't lock up human beings like you're in a zoo. Personally, I would let the animals go, too.[30]

28. Kelly, *Other Lands Have Dreams*, 149.
29. Kelly, interview, 31.
30. Ibid., 12.

The Violence of the U.S. Military and Prisons

The United States now incarcerates 2.1 million people—more than any other country—at a rate that has quadrupled over the last twenty-five years. On average the nation spends $33,000 annually on each prisoner. The United States is also ranked number one in the international sales of weapons. Part three of Kelly's book, *Other Lands Have Dreams,* contains letters from prison, many of which draw connections between poverty in the United States and the country's wars with other nations. Building prisons and making wars are based on the idea that punishment and retribution can beneficially change people's behavior. Jesus pointed to an alternative to moral judgment and retribution when he challenged the "eye-for-an-eye, tooth-for-a-tooth" philosophy and offered his teachings on active suffering ("turn the other cheek"), on compassion ("love your enemy"), on self-control ("do unto others as you would have done to you"), and noncooperation with violence ("resist not evil").

> Military and prison structures don't train recruits to view "the enemy" or "the inmate" as precious and valuable humans deserving forgiveness, mercy, and respect, even if they have trespassed against us. These systems don't foster the notion that we ourselves could be mistaken, that we might seek forgiveness, or that we might, together with presumed outcasts, create a better world. Look to Scriptures for such views—they're there—but don't expect love of enemy and the Golden Rule to guide military, prison, or intelligence systems anywhere in the world.[31]

Kelly's experience in prison has led her to raise her voice against the violent foundations of the U.S. prison system, an institution that has made an enemy of the poor. By entering prisons, war zones, and ghettoes, we follow in the footsteps of Jesus, who lived with and loved the poor, the ill, and the oppressed.

> Not all peace activists can be part of civil disobedience actions resulting in prison sentences. But for those who can, entering the prisons offers an opportunity to bet-

31. *Other Lands Have Dreams*, 102.

ter understand how the once lauded war on poverty has become a war against the poor.[32]

Most of the women that Kelly met in prison had been arrested while trying to escape difficult circumstances through drug use, drug sales, or both. She notes that 78 percent of all prisoners are doing time for drug-related crimes and that over half are punished for nonviolent crimes. Kelly saw firsthand that punishing prisoners cultivates anger and fear and leads to more violence.

> The cruel flaw in the prison system lies in the intent to punish people rather than help them.[33]

A direct material link between the U.S. military and prison systems is the manufacturing of military and security goods by prisoners. Federal Prison Industries Inc., also known as UNICOR, was created in 1934 under President Franklin Roosevelt. At Pekin Prison, female prisoners help make small cages to transport children caught by immigration authorities. They also make armored plates for U.S. military Humvees. These prison laborers earn between 23 cents and $1.23 per hour. Kelly challenges the belief that violent people require punitive imprisonment, offering the Catholic Worker model as an alternative.

> Some say that the prison system is necessary so that society can isolate abusive people from defenseless victims. That's not true. Abusive people can be separated from victims and helped to cope with their sick behavior without losing every other human freedom. Again, the Catholic Worker Houses of Hospitality come to mind. Working as volunteers, seeking merely the chance to join communities dedicated to the works of mercy and simple living, hundreds of idealistic, kindly people have set up havens for their fellow human beings, aiming to treat them as guests and together form community. At no cost to U.S. taxpayers, these communities have been replicated in many of the neediest sections of urban and rural America.[34]

32. *Other Lands Have Dreams*, 94.
33. Ibid., 95.
34. Ibid., 96.

Don't Be Afraid
(Courage is Contagious)

> Courage is the ability to control your fear and courage is contagious. I'd add to those definitions an additional truism that can help dissolve fear: treat other people right, and you won't have to be afraid of them.[35]

Relaxing fear and anger, and transforming these emotions into courage and love are the keys to nonviolent Christian peacemaking. The life and teachings of Jesus provide vivid examples of how to engage in this creative process. By witnessing war and holding dying Iraqi children in her arms, Kathy Kelly has faced fear and transformed it into courage.

> I have found myself wanting to identify with a little teenager who was garbed in a loincloth and in the fourteenth chapter of the Gospel of Mark, tries to stay with Jesus up to the very end. In the Gospel of Mark there is a lot of emphasis on Jesus being abandoned. Even on the cross he says, "My God, my God, why have *you* forsaken me?" And that is after the relatives and the friends and disciples and followers have all gone. But there is this kid who tries to hang in there to the end. The soldiers go to grab the child, a young boy. He runs away, the loincloth comes undone, the soldiers have the loincloth and he's stark naked. And nakedness was as much a sign of humiliation then as it would be in Abu Ghraib now, in that culture. But then when the women come to the tomb after Jesus has been crucified, as the Markan community expresses it, the young boy, fully matured and dressed in a long white gown, is there. And his first words to the women are, "Don't be afraid."[36]

To be aware of our anger and of the circumstances that allow it to rise, and not to be reactionary or to act upon that anger, is truly revolutionary and integral to Christian peacemaking. During

---

35. *Other Lands Have Dreams*, 27.
36. Kelly, interview, 5.

her experience of the "shock-and-awe" bombing of Baghdad, Kelly directed her anger into nonviolent actions.

> Yes, we are angry, very angry, and yet we feel deep responsibility to further the nonviolent antiwar efforts that burgeon in cities and towns throughout the world. We can direct our anger toward clear confrontation, controlling it so that we won't explode in reactionary rage, but rather draw the sympathies of people toward the plight of innocent people here who never wanted to attack the U.S., who wonder, even as the bombs terrify them, why they can't live as brothers and sisters with people in America.[37]

Kelly has also seen the power of forgiveness to transform violent emotions and actions. In the wake of the attacks of September 11, 2001, and the subsequent wars on Iraq and Afghanistan, she invites people in the United States to consider a "widening of the space," through understanding and compassion.[38] Kelly joined families and friends of people who were killed in the 9/11 attacks to display banners at the White House that read: "Our grief is not a call for war."

> The role of forgiveness as something that would interrupt the spirals of violence is, of course, crucial. To be able to say, "Yes, I loved this person and my arms will ache emptily for a person who will never return. But I don't want to impose that suffering on another person. And, in fact, I want to try to understand or be part of that other person's culture." That is an extraordinary demand, but is one in which I would place a great deal of hope. I think that when there is some widening of the space wherein people could come together without killing one another, there is logically a better possibility for that hope to develop in very concrete ways.[39]

Relaxing fear allows us to see our own actions and the actions of our country as they really are, and to see its history of violence as well as the current suffering resulting from its policies and actions.

37. Kelly, *Other Lands Have Dreams*, 67.
38. Kelly, interview, 33.
39. Ibid.

Kathy Kelly reminds us that each of us plays a part in peacemaking in the world; we are all agents of change.

> Change is coming. Light as the breath of excruciatingly beautiful Iraqi children nearing their deaths, demanding as the imploring eyes of their mothers who asked us why . . . you can feel it coming.[40]

40. Kelly, *Other Lands Have Dreams*, 104.

References

Chapter 1: "Contemporary Violence Necessitates Christian Nonviolent Peacemaking"

Easwaran, Eknath. *Gandhi the Man.* Petaluma, CA: Nilgiri, 1972.

Gandhi, Mahatma. *Nonviolence in Peace and War.* Ahmedebad, India: Navajivan Trust, 1948.

Gilligan, James. *Preventing Violence.* London: Thames & Hudson, 1996.

King, Martin Luther, Jr.. *Stride Toward Freedom.* New York: Harper, 1958.

Straus, Murray. *Beating the Devil Out of Them: Corporal Punishment in American Children.* New Jersey: Transaction Books, 2001.

Chapter 2: "Creating Peace: Jesus and Nonviolence"

Easwaran, Eknath. *Gandhi the Man.* Petaluma, CA:. Nilgiri Press, 1972.

———. *The Dhammapada.* Translated with an introduction by Eknath Easwaran. Petaluma, CA: Nilgiri, 1986.

Gandhi, Mahatma. *What Jesus Means to Me.* Ahmedabad, India.: Navajivan Trust, 1924

———. *Nonviolence in Peace and War.* Ahmedabad, India:. Navajivan Trust, 1948.

Jones, Alexander et al., translators. *The Jerusalem Bible.* Garden City, NY: Doubleday, 1966.

King, Martin Luther, Jr. *Why We Can't Wait.* New York: Signet, 1964.

Merton, Thomas. *The Seven Storey Mountain.* New York: Harcourt, Brace, 1948.

———. *Gandhi On Nonviolence.* New York: New Directions, 1965.

Palmer, G., Sherrard, P., and Ware, K., translators. *The Philokalia.* London: Faber and Faber, 1984.

Washington, James Melvin. *A Testament of Hope: The Essential Writings and Speeches of Martin Luther King, Jr.* San Francisco: Harper and Row, 1991.

Chapter 3: "Jones, Kelly, and the Quakers"

Fosdick, Harry. *Rufus Jones Speaks to Our Time.* New York: Macmillan, 1954.

Griffin, Emilie, and Douglas V. Steere, editors. *Quaker Spirituality: Selected Writings.* Foreword by Rick Moody. San Francisco: Harper San Francisco, 2005.

Jones, Rufus. "The Mystic's Experience of God." *Atlantic Monthly* 128 (1921) 637–45.

———. "Lighted Lives." In *The Luminous Trail*, 147–53. New York: Macmillan, 1947.

———. *The Luminous Trail*. New York: Macmillan, 1947.

Kelly, Thomas. *Holy Obedience*. Philadelphia: Quaker Pamphlets, 1939.

——— "Holy Obedience." In *A Testament of Devotion* 23–48. New York: Harper and Row, 1941.

———. *A Testament of Devotion*. New York: Harper and Row, 1941.

———. *The Eternal Promise*. New York: Harper and Row, 1966.

Merton, Thomas. *Gandhi on Non-Violence*. Edited with an introduction by Thomas Merton; preface by Mark Kurlansky. New York: New Directions, 2007.

Chapter 4: "Martin Luther King Jr."

Easwaran, Eknath. *Gandhi, the Man: The Story of His Transformation*. 3d edition. Foreword by Michael Nagler. Afterword by Timothy Flinders. Tomales, CA: Nilgiri, 1997.

King, Martin Luther, Jr. *Stride Toward Freedom*. New York: Harper, 1958.

———. "The Most Durable Power" (1958a). In *A Testament of Hope: The Essential Writings and Speeches of Martin Luther King Jr.*, edited by James Melvin Washington, 10–11. San Francisco: Harper and Row, 1991.

———. "The Power of Nonviolence" (1958b). In *A Testament of Hope: The Essential Writings and Speeches of Martin Luther King Jr.*, edited by James Melvin Washington, 12–15. San Francisco: Harper and Row, 1991.

———. "An Experiment in Love: Nonviolent Resistance" (1958c). In *A Testament of Hope: The Essential Writings and Speeches of Martin Luther King Jr.*, edited by James Melvin Washington 16–20. San Francisco: Harper and Row, 1991.

———. "Nonviolence and Racial Justice" (1957). In *A Testament of Hope: The Essential Writings and Speeches of Martin Luther King Jr.*, edited by James Melvin Washington 5–9. San Francisco: Harper and Row, 1991.

———. "My Trip to the Land of Gandhi" (1959). In *A Testament of Hope: The Essential Writings and Speeches of Martin Luther King Jr.*, edited by James Melvin Washington, 23–30. San Francisco: Harper and Row, 1991.

———. *Why We Can't Wait*. New York. Signet, 1964.

———. "Love, Law, and Civil Disobedience" (1961a). In *A Testament of Hope: The Essential Writings and Speeches of Martin Luther King Jr.*, edited by James Melvin Washington, 43–53. San Francisco: Harper and Row, 1991.

———. *I Have a Dream* [1963]. New York: Scholastic, 1997.

———. "Nobel Prize Acceptance Speech" (1964). In *A Testament of Hope: The Essential Writings and Speeches of Martin Luther King Jr.*, edited by James Melvin Washington, 224–26. San Francisco: Harper and Row, 1991.

————. "Next Stop: The North" (1965). In *A Testament of Hope: The Essential Writings and Speeches of Martin Luther King Jr.*, edited by James Melvin Washington,189–94. San Francisco: Harper and Row, 1991.

————. "Nonviolence: The Only Road to Freedom" (1966). In *A Testament of Hope: The Essential Writings and Speeches of Martin Luther King Jr.*, edited by James Melvin Washington, 54–61. San Francisco: Harper and Row, 1991.

————. "Showdown for Nonviolence" (1968a). In *A Testament of Hope: The Essential Writings and Speeches of Martin Luther King Jr.*, edited by James Melvin Washington, 64–74. San Francisco: Harper and Row, 1991.

————. "The Drum Major Instinct" (1968b). In *A Testament of Hope: The Essential Writings and Speeches of Martin Luther King Jr.*, edited by James Melvin Washington, 259–67. San Francisco: Harper and Row, 1991.

————. "Remaining Awake through a Great Revolution" (1968c). In *A Testament of Hope: The Essential Writings and Speeches of Martin Luther King Jr.*, edited by James Melvin Washington, 268–78. San Francisco: Harper and Row, 1991.

Washington, James Melvin. *A Testament of Hope: The Essential Writings and Speeches of Martin Luther King, Jr.* San Francisco: Harper and Row, 1991.

Chapter 5: "Dorothy Day and the *Catholic Worker*"

Day, Dorothy. *The Long Loneliness. The Autobiography of Dorothy Day.* San Francisco:. Harper and Row, 1952.

Forest, James H. *Love Is the Measure: A Biography of Dorothy Day.* Revised edition. Orbis: Maryknoll, NY 1994.

Chapter 6: "Thomas Merton"

Forest, James H. *Living with Wisdom; A Life of Thomas Merton.* Maryknoll, NY: Orbis, 1991.

Merton, Thomas. *New Seeds of Contemplation.* New York: New Directions, 1961.

————. *Raids on the Unspeakable.* A New Directions Paperback. New York: New Directions, 1966.

————. *Gandhi on Non-Violence.* New York: New Directions, 1965.

————. *Faith and Violence: Christian Teaching and Christian Practice.* Notre Dame: University of Notre Dame Press, 1968.

————. *Contemplative Prayer.* Garden City, NY: Image, 1971.

————. *The Nonviolent Alternative.* Revised edition of *Thomas Merton on Peace.* New York: Farrar, Straus, and Giroux, 1980.

Chapter 7: "Jim Douglass"

Douglass, James W. 2005. Interview by John Malkin. July 6. Audio recording. Free Radio Santa Cruz, Santa Cruz, California.

———. *The Nonviolent Coming of God*. Reprint, Eugene, OR: Wipf and Stock, 2006.

———. "A Letter to the American People (and Myself in Particular) on the Unspeakable." No pages. Accessed January 8, 2008. Online: http:// www. maryferrell.org /mffweb/archive/viewer/showDoc.do?docId=1723

Chapter 8: "Kathy Kelly"

Kelly, Kathy. *Other Lands Have Dreams: From Baghdad to Pekin Prison*. Oakland, CA: Counterpunch, AK, 2005.

———.2005. Interview by John Malkin. May 23. Transcript of Audio recording. Salinas, California.

Bibliography

Abel, David. "U. S. Arms Training Aided Milosevic." *Boston Globe*, July 4, 1999, A10. Accessed January 8, 2008. Online: http://davidabel5.blogspot.com/

Albright, Madeleine. 1996. Interview by Lesley Stahl, *60 Minutes*, CBS. May 12.

Amnesty International. "Death Penalty: Death Sentences and Executions in 2006." Accessed January 4, 2008. Online: http://www.amnesty.org/en/death-penalty/death-sentences-and-executions-in-2006.

———. *Death Penalty News*, July 2007. Accessed January 8, 2008. Online: http://www.amnesty.org/en/alfresco_asset/f7a04292-a2a9-11dc-8d74-6f4 5f39984e5/act530012007en.html.

Archer, Dane, and Rosemary Gartner. *Violence and Crime in Cross-National Perspective*. New Haven: Yale University Press, 1984.

Arms Trade Resource Center. "U.S. Weapons at War: Promoting Freedom or Fueling Conflict?" No pages. Accessed January 3, 2008. Online: http://www.worldpolicy .org/projects/arms/reports/PRWaW052505.html.

Aslam, Abid. "U.S. Selling More Weapons to Undemocratic Regimes That Support 'War on Terror.'" News Release. May 25, 2005. No pages. Accessed January 3, 2008. Online: http://www.commondreams.org/headlines05/0525-04.htm.

Associated Press. "2007 Becomes Deadliest Yet For U.S. in Iraq." Accessed: January 3, 2008. Online: http://www.msnbc.msn.com/id/21650614/.

"Atom Bomb Row Minister Apologises." Accessed January 3, 2008. Online: http://news.bbc.co.uk/2/hi/asia-pacific/6258190.stm.

BBC. "1954: US Tests Atomic Bomb in Bikini." No pages. Accessed January 4, 2008. Online: http://news.bbc.co.uk/onthisday/hi/dates/stories /march /1/ newsid_2781000/2781419.stm.

Bagdikian, Ben H. *The New Media Monopoly*. Boston: Beacon, 2004.

Bailey, Rea. "Study Links TV Viewing among Kids to Later Violence." *CNN*, March 28, 2002. Accessed January 7, 2008. Online: http://archives.cnn .com/ 2002/HEALTH /parenting/03/28/kids.tv.violence/index.html.

Ballou, Adin. *Christian Non-Resistance*. Blackstone edition. Philadelphia: McKin, 1846.

Barnaby, Frank. "The Effects of the Atomic Bombings of Hiroshima and Nagasaki." In *Hiroshima and Nagasaki: Retrospect and Prospect*, edited by Douglas Holdstock and Frank Barnaby, 1–9. London: Cass, 1995.

Bennett, Larone, Jr. *Before the Mayflower: A History of Black America*. 6th edition. Chicago: Johnson, 1988.

Berrigan, Daniel. Introduction to *The Long Loneliness: The Autobiography of Dorothy Day*, i–xxiii.

Berrigan, Frida. "The War Profiteers: How Are Weapons Manufacturers Faring in the War?" *Arms Trade Resource Center*, Current Updates: December 17,

2001. Accessed January 7, 2008. Online: http: //www.worldpolicy.org/ projects/ arms /updates /profiteers121701.html.

Bryers, Gavin, performer. *Jesus' Blood Never Failed Me Yet.* 438832-2 Point.© Point Music, 1993.

Burnham, Gilbert, Riyadh Lafta, et al. "Mortality after the 2003 Invasion of Iraq: A Cross-Sectional Cluster Sample Survey." Abstract. *The Lancet* 368 (2006) 1421–28. Abstract. Accessed January 8, 2008. Online: http:// www.thelancet .com /journals /lancet /article /PIIS0140673606694919/abstract.

"Catholic Worker Movement." No pages. Accessed December 17, 2007. Online: http://www.catholicworker.org/index.cfm.

CBS News and the Associated Press. "Rumsfeld: Worst Still to Come." News release. May 7, 2004. Accessed January 8, 2008. Online: http://www.cbs news.com/stories/2004/05/08/iraq/main616338.shtml.

Children's Defense Fund. "Protect Children Instead of Guns. September 2002." Accessed: January 3, 2008. Online: http://www .childrensdefense.org /site / PageServer? pagename=education_gunviolence_factsheets_protectchildren.

Chomsky, Noam. *Hegemony or Survival: America's Quest for Global Dominance.* New York: Metropolitan, 2003.

———. *Necessary Illusions: Thought Control in Democratic Societies.* Boston: South End, 1989.

Coles, Robert. *Dorothy Day: A Radical Devotion.* Radcliffe Biography Series. Reading, MA: Addison, 1987.

Commager, Henry Steele. *Crusaders for Freedom.* Illustrated by Mimi Korach. Garden City, NY: Doubleday, 1962.

Dalai Lama XIV. *The Good Heart: A Buddhist Perspective on the Teachings of Jesus,* edited with a preface by Robert Kiely. Boston: Wisdom, 1996.

———. *How to Practice: The Way to a Meaningful Life.* New York: Pocket, 2002.

———. *Training the Mind.* Accessed February 21, 2008. Online http://www.dal ailama.com/.

Darrow, Clarence. *Resist Not Evil.* Montclair, NJ: Patterson Smith, 1972.

Day, Dorothy. *House of Hospitality.* New York: Sheed & Ward, 1939.

———. *Loaves and Fishes.* New York: Harper & Row, 1963.

———. *The Long Loneliness: The Autobiography of Dorothy Day.* San Francisco: Harper and Row, 1952.

———. *On Pilgrimage.* New York: Catholic Worker, 1948.

———. *Therese.* Springfield, IL: Templegate, 1979.

Dobyns, Henry F. "Estimating Aboriginal American Population: An Appraisal of Techniques with a New Hemispheric Estimate." *Current Anthropology* 7 (1966) 395–416.

Douglass, James W. "A Letter to the American People (and Myself in Particular) on the Unspeakable." No pages. Accessed January 8, 2008. Online: http:// www.maryferrell.org /mffweb/archive/viewer/showDoc.do?docId=1723.

———.2005. Interview by John Malkin. July 6. Tape recording. Free Radio Santa Cruz, Santa Cruz, California.

———. *Lightning East to West: Jesus, Gandhi, and the Nuclear Age.* Reprint, Eugene, OR: Wipf and Stock, 2006.

———. *The Non-Violent Cross: A Theology of Revolution and Peace.* Reprint, Eugene, OR: Wipf and Stock, 2006.

———. *The Nonviolent Coming of God.* Reprint, Eugene, OR: Wipf and Stock, 2006.

———. *Resistance and Contemplation: The Way of Liberation.* New York: Doubleday, 1972. Reprint, Eugene, OR: Wipf and Stock, 2006.

Easwaran, Eknath. *The Dhammapada,* translated with a general introduction by Eknath Easwaran. Petaluma, CA: Nigiri, 1986.

———. *Gandhi, the Man: The Story of His Transformation.* 3d edition. Foreword by Michael Nagler. Afterword by Timothy Flinders. Tomales, CA: Nilgiri, 1997.

Egan, Eileen. *Dorothy Day and the Permanent Revolution.* Erie, PA: Benet, 1983.

Einstein, Albert. *Einstein on Peace.* Edited by Otto Nathan and Heinz Norden; preface by Bertrand Russell. New York: Avenel, 1981.

Ellsberg, Robert. *Dorothy Day, Selected Writings: By Little and by Little.* Maryknoll: Orbis, 2005.

Forest, James H. *Living with Wisdom; A Life of Thomas Merton.* Maryknoll: Orbis, 1991.

———. *Love Is the Measure: A Biography of Dorothy Day.* Revised edition. Maryknoll, NY: Orbis, 1994.

Fosdick, Harry Emerson. *Rufus Jones Speaks to Our Time, an Anthology.* New York: Macmillan, 1951.

Frank, Andrew. *The Routledge Historical Atlas of the American South.* Routledge Atlases of American History. New York: Routledge, 1999.

Friends Committee on National Legislation. "Issues: Military Spending: 41% of Your Taxes Go to War." Accessed January 4, 2008. Online: http:// www .fcnl .org /issues /item .php?item_id= 2336&issue _id=19.

Gandhi, Mathama. *All Men Are Brothers: Autobiographical Reflections.* Compiled and edited by Krishna Kripalani. New York: Continuum, 1988.

———. *An Autobiography: The Story of My Experiments with Truth.* Boston: Beacon, 1940.

———. *Gandhi on Non-Violence: Selected Texts from Mahandas K. Gadnhi's "Non-Violence in Peace and War."* Edited with an introduction by Thomas Merton; preface by Mark Kurlansky. New York: New Directions, 2007.

———. *Nonviolence in Peace and War.* Ahmedebad, India: Navajivan Trust, 1948.

———. *What Jesus Means to Me.* Ahmedebad, India.: Navajivan Trust, 1924.

Gilligan, James. *Preventing Violence.* London: Thames & Hudson, 2001.

———. *Violence: Reflections on a National Epidemic.* New York: Vintage, 1997.

———. *Violence: Our Deadly Epidemic and Its Causes.* New York: Putnam, 1996.

Griffin, Emilie, and Douglas V. Steere, editors. *Quaker Spirituality: Selected Writings.* Foreword by Rick Moody. San Francisco: Harper San Francisco, 2005.

Grimmett, Richard F. *Conventional Arms Transfers to Developing Nations, 1997–2004.* RL33051. Washington DC: Congressional Research Service, August 29, 2005. Accessed January 3, 2008. Online: http://www.opencrs.com/document/RL33051.

Grisbrooke, W. Jardine, editor. *The Spiritual Counsels of Fr. John of Kronstadt.* Cambridge: James Clarke, 1981.

Grossman, Dave. On Killing: The Psychological Cost of Learning to Kill in War and Society. Boston: Little, Brown and Company, 1995.

Grossman, Zoltan, compiler. "A Century of U.S. Military Interventions: From Wounded Knee to Afghanistan." Accessed January 4, 2008. Online: http://www .zmag .org /CrisesCurEvts/interventions.htm.

Harding, Dr. Vincent. Martin Luther King: *The Inconvenient Hero.* New York: Orbis, 1996

Hedges, Chris. *What Every Person Should Know about War.* New York: Free, 2003.

Hellman, Christopher. "America Spending More on Security Than Most Know." Originally published in Topeka *Capital-Journal,* November 16, 2007. Accessed January 4, 2008. Online: http: //www.armscontrolcenter.org/ policy/ securityspending/ articles /spending_more_than_most_know/.

Jahn, Gunnar. Speech at the presentation of the Nobel Peace Award for 1947. Oslo, Norway, December 10, 1947. Accessed February 19, 2008. Online: http://www.afsc.org/about/nobel/gunnarjahnspeech.htm.

Jamail, Dahr. *Beyond the Green Zone: Dispatches from an Unembedded Journalist in Occupied Iraq,* Chicago: Haymarket, 2007.

Johnson, Jeffrey G., et al. "Television Viewing and Aggressive Behavior during Adolescence and Adulthood." Abstract. *Science* 295 (2002) 2468. Accessed January 7, 2008. Online: http://www.sciencemag.org/cgi/content/abstract/295/5564/2468.

Jones, Alexander et al., translators. *The Jerusalem Bible.* Garden City, NY: Doubleday, 1966.

Jones, Rufus. *Finding the Trail of Life.* New York: Macmillan, 1943.

———. "Lighted Lives." In *The Luminous Trail,* 147–53. New York: Macmillan, 1947.

———. *The Luminous Trail.* New York: Macmillan, 1947.

———. "The Mystic's Experience of God." *Atlantic Monthly* 128 (1921) 637–45.

Kadloubovsky, E., and G. E. H. Palmer, translators. *Unseen Warfare: The Spiritual Combat and Path to Paradise of Lorenzo Scupoli.* Crestwood, NY: St. Vladimir's Seminary Press, 1987.

Kelly, Kathy. 2005. Interview by John Malkin. May 23. Transcript of tape recording. Salinas, California.

———. *Other Lands Have Dreams: From Baghdad to Pekin Prison*, foreword by Milan Rai. Petrolia, CA: CounterPunch, 2005.

Kelly, Thomas R. *The Eternal Promise*. New York: Harper and Row, 1966.

———. *Holy Obedience*. Philadelphia: Quaker Pamphlets, 1939.

———. "Holy Obedience." In *A Testament of Devotion*, 23–48. New York: Harper, 1941.

Kempe, Frederick. "The Ties That Blind: U.S. Taught Noriega to Spy, but Pupil Has His Own Agenda." *Wall Street Journal*, October 18, 1989, A1 and A20.

King, Martin Luther, Jr. "An Address Before the National Press Club." In *A Testament of Hope: The Essential Writings and Speeches of Martin Luther King, Jr.*, edited by James Melvin Washington, 99–104. San Francisco: Harper and Row, 1991.

———. "The American Dream." In *A Testament of Hope: The Essential Writings and Speeches of Martin Luther King Jr.*, edited by James Melvin Washington, 208–16. San Francisco: Harper and Row, 1991.

———. "A Christmas Sermon on Peace." In *A Testament of Hope: The Essential Writings and Speeches of Martin Luther King Jr.*, edited by James Melvin Washington, 253–58. San Francisco: Harper and Row, 1991.

———. "The Drum Major Instinct." In *A Testament of Hope: The Essential Writings and Speeches of Martin Luther King Jr.*, edited by James Melvin Washington, 259–67. San Francisco: Harper and Row, 1991.

———. "An Experiment in Love: Nonviolent Resistance." In *A Testament of Hope: The Essential Writings and Speeches of Martin Luther King Jr.*, edited by James Melvin Washington 16–20. San Francisco: Harper and Row, 1991.

———. *I Have a Dream*. New York: Scholastic, 1997.

———. "I See the Promised Land." In *A Testament of Hope: The Essential Writings and Speeches of Martin Luther King Jr.*, edited by James Melvin Washington, 279–88. San Francisco: Harper and Row, 1991.

———. "Love, Law, and Civil Disobedience." In *A Testament of Hope: The Essential Writings and Speeches of Martin Luther King Jr.*, edited by James Melvin Washington, 43–53. San Francisco: Harper and Row, 1991.

———. "The Most Durable Power." In *A Testament of Hope: The Essential Writings and Speeches of Martin Luther King Jr.*, edited by James Melvin Washington, 10–11. San Francisco: Harper and Row, 1991.

———. "My Trip to the Land of Gandhi." In *A Testament of Hope: The Essential Writings and Speeches of Martin Luther King Jr.*, edited by James Melvin Washington, 23–30. San Francisco: Harper and Row, 1991.

———. "Next Stop: The North." In *A Testament of Hope: The Essential Writings and Speeches of Martin Luther King Jr.*, edited by James Melvin Washington,189–94. San Francisco: Harper and Row, 1991.

———. "Nobel Prize Acceptance Speech." In *A Testament of Hope: The Essential Writings and Speeches of Martin Luther King Jr.*, edited by James Melvin Washington, 224–26. San Francisco: Harper and Row, 1991.

————. "Nonviolence and Racial Justice." In *A Testament of Hope: The Essential Writings and Speeches of Martin Luther King Jr.*, edited by James Melvin Washington 5–9. San Francisco: Harper and Row, 1991.

————. "Nonviolence: The Only Road to Freedom." In *A Testament of Hope: The Essential Writings and Speeches of Martin Luther King Jr.*, edited by James Melvin Washington, 54–61. San Francisco: Harper and Row, 1991.

————. "The Power of Nonviolence." In *A Testament of Hope: The Essential Writings and Speeches of Martin Luther King Jr.*, edited by James Melvin Washington, 12–15. San Francisco: Harper and Row, 1991.

————."Remaining Awake through a Great Revolution." In *A Testament of Hope: The Essential Writings and Speeches of Martin Luther King Jr.*, edited by James Melvin Washington, 268–78. San Francisco: Harper and Row, 1991.

————. "Showdown for Nonviolence." In *A Testament of Hope: The Essential Writings and Speeches of Martin Luther King Jr.*, edited by James Melvin Washington, 64–74. San Francisco: Harper and Row, 1991.

————. *Strength to Love*. Philadelphia: Fortress, 1981.

————. *Stride toward Freedom*. New York: Harper, 1958.

————. *A Testament of Hope: The Essential Writings and Speeches of Martin Luther King, Jr.*, edited by James Melvin Washington. San Francisco: Harper and Row, 1991.

————. "A Time to Break Silence." In *A Testament of Hope: The Essential Writings and Speeches of Martin Luther King Jr.*, edited by James Melvin Washington, 231–44. San Francisco: Harper and Row, 1991.

————. *Why We Can't Wait*. New York: Signet, 1964.

Kirsch, Steven J. *Children, Adolescents and Media Violence: A Critical Look at the Research*. Thousand Oaks, CA: Sage, 2006.

Merton, Thomas. *Contemplative Prayer*. Garden City: Image, 1971.

————. *Faith and Violence: Christian Teaching and Christian Practice*. Notre Dame: Notre Dame University Press, 1968.

————. *Mystics and Zen Masters*. New York: Farrar, Straus, and Giroux, 1967.

————. *New Seeds of Contemplation*. New York: New Directions, 1961.

————. *The Nonviolent Alternative*. Revised edition of *Thomas Merton on Peace*. New York: Farrar, Straus, and Giroux, 1980.

————. *Raids on the Unspeakable*. A New Directions Paperback. New York: New Directions, 1966.

————. *The Seven Storey Mountain*. New York: Harcourt, Brace, Jovanovich. 1948.

————. "Gandhi and the One-Eyed Giant." In *Gandhi on Non-Violence*. Edited with an introduction by Thomas Merton; preface by Mark Kurlansky, 1–22. New York: New Directions, 2007.

Merton, Thomas, editor. *Gandhi on Non-Violence*. New York: New Directions, 2007.

Miller, William D. *Dorothy Day: A Biography*. San Francisco: Harper & Row, 1982.

―――. *A Harsh and Dreadful Love: Dorothy Day and the Catholic Worker Movement.* With new photos and a foreword by Phillip M. Runkel. New York: Liveright, 1973.

Moulton, Phillips P., editor. *The Journal and Major Essays of John Woolman.* Richmond, IN: Friends United, 2000.

Nagler, Michael. *The Search for a Nonviolent Future: A Promise of Peace for Ourselves, Our Families and Our World.* Revised and updated. Maui: Inner Ocean, 2004.

―――. 1999. Interview by John Malkin. October 11. Tape recording. University of California–Berkeley.

―――. *Living Buddha, Living Christ;* introduction by Elaine Pagels; foreword by David Steindl-Rast. New York: Riverhead, 1995.

―――. *Love in Action: Writings on Nonviolent Social Change.* Berkeley: Parallax, 1993.

National Education Association Health Information Network. "Statistics: Gun Violence in Our Communities." Accessed January 3, 2008. Online: http: //www.neahin.org /programs/schoolsafety/gunsafety/statistics.htm.

Nhat Hanh, Thich. *Miracle of Mindfulness!: A Manual for Meditation.* Translated by Mobi Warren. Boston: Beacon, 1976.

Nickalls, John L., editor. *The Journal of George Fox.* Cambridge: Cambridge University Prses, 1952.

O'Grady, Jim. *Dorothy Day: With Love for the Poor.* Staten Island, NY: Ward Hill, 1993.

Palmer, G. E. H., Philip Sherrard, and Kallistos Ware, translators and editors. *The Philokalia: The Complete Text.* London: Faber and Faber, 1984.

Parrish, Geov. MoJo Wire. "U.S. Arms Exporters: General Electric." Action Atlas. *Mother Jones.* Accessed January 4, 2008. Online: http:// www.motherjones .com /news /special_reports/arms/ge.html.

Pilgrim, Peace. *Peace Pilgrim: Her Life and Work in Her Own Words,* compiled by some of her friends. Santa Fe, NM: Ocean Tree, 1982.

"Profits of War." Extract from *The Halliburton Agenda: The Politics of Oil and Money,* by Dan Briodi. *Guardian,* July 22, 2004.

Rao, K. L. Seshagiri. *Mahatma Gandhi and Comparative Religion.* 2d edition. Dehli: Bandarssidass, 1990.

Reuters. "U.S. Soldiers' Suicide Rate in Iraq Doubles in 2005." News release. December 19, 2006. No pages. Accessed January 4, 2008. Online: http:// www.alertnet.org/thenews/newsdesk/N19303337.htm.

Roberts, Nancy. *Dorothy Day and the Catholic Worker.* Albany: State University of New York Press, 1984.

Rogers, Carl R. *Client-Centered Therapy: Its Current Practice, Implications and Theory._*Boston: Houghton Mifflin, 1951.

―――. "The Necessary and Sufficient Conditions of Therapeutic Personality Change." *Journal of Consulting Psychology* 21 (1957) 95–103.

―――. *On Becoming a Person: A Therapist's View of Psychotherapy.* Boston: Houghton Mifflin, 1961.

Rosenberg, Marshall. *Nonviolent Communication: A Language of Life.* Encinitas, CA: Puddle Dancer, 2003.

Roszak. Theodore. *Person/Planet.* Garden City, NY: Anchor, 1978.

Saunders, Doug. "Military Training Links String of Serial Killers." *Toronto Globe and Mail,* October 28, 2002, A-5.

Scheer, Robert. "Bush's Faustian Deal with the Taliban." *San Francisco Chronicle,* May 24, 2001.

Shah, Anup. "World Military Spending." Accessed January 4, 2008. Online: http://www.globalissues.org/Geopolitics/ArmsTrade/Spending.asp.

Sharp, Gene. *The Methods of Nonviolent Action.* Boston: Extending Horizons, 1973.

Shaw, I. *Tales of the Dervishes.* New York: E. P. Dutton, 1967.

Sophrony, Archimandrite. *Saint Silouan, the Athonite.* Athense: St. Vladimir's Seminary Press, 1999.

Stannard, David E. *American Holocaust: The Conquest of the New World.* New York: Oxford University Press, 1993.

Tait, Paul. "Three US Troops Killed in Iraq, Blast in Baghdad." News release. November 14, 2007. Reuters. Accessed January 4, 2008. Online: http://www .javno.com /en/world /clanak.php?id=98034.

Toffler, Alvin, and Heidi Toffler. *War and Anti-War: Survival at the Dawn of the Twenty-First Century.* Boston: Little, Brown, 1993.

Tolstoy, Leo. *The Kingdom of God Is Within You: Christianity Not as a Mystic Religion but as a New Theory of Life.* New York: Cassell, 1894.

United Nations Department of Disarmament Affairs. *The Relationship between Disarmament and Development in the International Context.* Report of the Secretary-General. New York: United Nations, 2004. Accessed January 4, 2008. Online: http://72.14.253.104/search?q=cache:WJqx1ljAaNQJ: disarmament.un.org/cab/D%26Dstudyseries31.doc+Stockholm+Intern ational+Peace+Research+Institute+%24950+billion&hl=en&ct=clnk&c d=10&gl=us.

United Nations Office of the High Commissioner of Human Rights. "Convention on the Prevention and Punishment of the Crime of Genocide, Paris, 9 December 1948. Entered into Force on 12 January 1951." *Treaty Series* London: H.M.S.O., 1970. Accessed January 8, 2008. Online: http://www.unhchr.ch/html/menu3/b/p_genoci.htm.

United Nations Office on Drugs and Crime. Division for Policy Analysis and Pubic Affairs. *Seventh United Nations Survey of Crime Trends and Operations of Criminal Justice Systems, Covering the Period 1998–2000.* Vienna: UNODC, 2001. Accessed January 4, 2008. Online: http://www.unodc.org/pdf/crime/ seventh_survey/7sc.pdf.

United States. Office of the Deputy Under Secretary of Defense (Installations and Environment). *Department of Defense Base Structure Report: Fiscal Year 2003 Baseline.* Washington DC: Office of the Deputy Under Secretary of Defense (Installations and Environment). Accessed January 4, 2008. Online: http:// www.defenselink.mil/news/Jun2003/basestructure2003.pdf.

United States Census Bureau. *Income, Poverty and Health Insurance Coverage in the United States: 2003.* Accessed January 7, 2008. Online: http: //www .census .gov/ prod /2004pubs/p60-226.pdf.

————. "Income Stable, Poverty Up, Numbers of Americans With and Without Health Insurance Rise, Census Bureau Reports." Press release. August 26. 2004. Accessed January 7, 2008. Online: http://www.census.gov/Press Release/www/releases/archives/income_wealth/002484.html.

Vining, Elizabeth Gray. *Friend of Life: A Biography of Rufus M. Jones.* New York: J. B. Lippincott, 1958.

Voices in the Wilderness. "Federal Judge Orders Fine Against US Citizens for Bringing Medicine to Iraq." News release, August 14, 2005. Accessed January 8, 2008. Online: http://www.vitw.org/archives/978.

Washington, James Melvin, editor. *A Testament of Hope: The Essential Writings and Speeches of Martin Luther King Jr.* San Francisco: Harper and Row, 1986.

War Resisters League. "Where Your Tax Income Really Goes." Accessed January 4, 2008. Online: http://www.warresisters.org/piechart.htm.

Werner, Tim. "Senate Unit Calls US 'Most Violent' Country on Earth," *Boston Globe*, March 13, 1991, 3.

Wilshire, B., editor. *William James: Essential Writings.* New York: SUNY Press, 1984.

Wink, Walter. *Jesus and Nonviolence: A Third Way.* Facets, Minneapolis: Augsburg Fortress, 2003.

————, editor. *Peace Is the Way: Writings on Nonviolence from the Fellowship of Reconciliation.* Maryknoll: Orbis, 2000.

Yang, Ni, and Daniel Linz. "Movie Ratings and the Context of Adult Videos: The Sex-Violence Ratio." *Journal of Communication* 40 (1990) 28–42.

Zinn, Howard *A People's History of the United States: 1492–Present.* New York: Harper Collins, 2003.

3/10